Maxine Clark's
ITALIAN
KITCHEN

Maxine Clark's
ITALIAN KITCHEN

simple steps to great
tasting Italian food

RYLAND
PETERS
& SMALL

LONDON NEW YORK

Dedication
I dedicate this book to everyone I have ever shared an Italian kitchen with, be they students, fellow chefs, or cooks, kitchen assistants, front-of-house or course managers, or just enthusiastic eaters and drinkers.

Design and photographic art direction
Steve Painter
Commissioning Editor Julia Charles
Production Hazel Kirkman
Publishing Director Alison Starling
Art Director Leslie Harrington

Prop Stylists Helen Trent, Roisin Nield
Food Stylists Maxine Clark, Linda Tubby
Indexer Hilary Bird

Author's acknowledgments
Firstly, grateful thanks and my admiration go to Julia Charles, my editor at Ryland Peters & Small for pulling this (and me) together, and for suggesting the book in the first place. Steve Painter, the designer of this book and photographic co-ordinator/art director. He is quite simply one of the best designers I have ever worked with. This was an immense task, and design-led from the beginning and he is responsible for all its gorgeous good looks. My appreciation for his hard work knows no bounds. As for the simply stunning photographs themselves, I have to thank two of my favorite photographers and friends, Martin Brigdale and Pete Cassidy. They capture the essence of the dishes in a cloak of magical light—thanks to you both. A photograph is nothing without the perfect background, plate, linen, or fork, and the irrepressible Helen Trent, despite battling ill health, kept her mind focussed on the evocative and gentle props used in many of the photogaphs. Thank you Helen. My thanks also go to assitants Sophie Wright and Suzy Plant (despite being very pregnant) for all their hard work and cheerfulness in the kitchen at the studio sessions.

First published in the United States in 2009 by Ryland, Peters & Small, Inc.
519 Broadway, 5th Floor
New York, NY 10012
www.rylandpeters.com

10 9 8 7 6 5 4 3 2 1

Text © Maxine Clark 2009
Design and photographs (see page 192)
© Ryland Peters & Small 2009

Some of the recipes in this book have been published previously by Ryland, Peters & Small in *Al Forno*, *Bruschetta*, *Flavors of Tuscany*, *Italian Salads*, *Italian Vegetables*, *Pizza*, *Risotto*, and *Trattoria*.

Library of Congress Cataloging-in-Publication Data

Clark, Maxine, 1955-
 [Italian kitchen]
 Maxine Clark's Italian kitchen : simple steps to great tasting Italian food.
     p. cm.
 Includes index.
 ISBN 978-1-84597-829-7
 1. Cookery, Italian. I. Title. II. Title: Italian kitchen.
  TX723.C56534 2009
  641.5945--dc22

2008044018

Printed and bound in China

Notes
- All spoon measurements are level unless otherwise stated.
- Herbs used in the recipes are fresh unless specified as dried.
- When a recipe calls for grated lemon peel buy unwaxed fruit and wash well before using. If you can only find treated fruit, scrub well in warm soapy water and rinse before using.
- Raw or partially cooked eggs should not be served to the very young or old, to pregnant women, or to anyone with a compromised immune system.
- Ovens should be preheated to the specified temperature. If using a fan-assisted oven, follow the manufacturer's instructions for adjusting cooking temperatures.

contents

introduction

I have been fortunate enough to cook, eat, teach, wash up, sing, make friends, share jokes, cry, and play in some wonderful Italian kitchens. In all of them I have learned, and am still learning, cooking techniques, Italian kitchen lore, and some very useful Italian words and phrases. All of them have one thing in common—they are kitchens with a big heart—and that sums up the Italian approach to food and cooking—shop, cook, and eat with a big generous heart!

I would like to describe a few of the kitchens that I have worked in. It was working in these kitchens that fired my passion for Italian food and cooking, coupled with the people I met in them—whether they were working there, visiting, or just popping in to say hello. They all had to have a say in what was being cooked and everyone had an opinion. And that is the root of my love of Italian food—the fact that food passionately matters to every Italian, it is in their being, it is part of life itself, it is to be shared and enjoyed with others. And it all starts in the kitchen.

The first kitchen I worked in was tiny, cluttered, very shabby, and idiosyncratic but everything I thought an Italian kitchen should be. It had a small gas stove that worked only when it felt like it, and a scrubbed wooden table that instantly felt like my best friend. Strangely, the hob was too high and the table too low, but I loved it. I could feel that only good things would come out of this kitchen, and I was right. Fresh egg pasta was made directly on the table, cut and filled and spread on flat baskets to dry off. Vegetables were griddled on ridged cast-iron pans set over the very particular gas burners—but once coaxed into action, produced memorable grilled zucchini, eggplant, bell peppers, and fennel. Joints of meat were seasoned, stuffed, rolled, and roasted in an oven that was almost impossible to get into, being crammed into a corner that almost didn't accommodate the open door. The oven had no light and by standing in front of it, your body blocked out any ambient light… but I got used to it and worked around the flaws. Somehow they didn't seem to matter—I was cooking in Italy, my dream. It was Michel Roux Jnr who said that a good chef can only blame himself for failure—not his oven or tools. It is the cook who makes a kitchen work. A kitchen, no matter how well-equipped, only responds to the cook inside it.

Walking into my next kitchen, I let out an audible gasp of delight. I could not believe my eyes. It seemed to be in a sort of half basement, with natural light streaming in from lofty windows. The walls were painted white and the floor and ceiling were terra cotta. The focus of the kitchen was a massive open stone fireplace with an ancient unglazed terra cotta tiled hearth. This was a fireplace that was meant for cooking in! Standing inside it and looking up the soot-black and delicious smelling chimney, I could see the tar-encrusted remnants of hooks and chains which had been used for hanging cauldrons and for smoking hams and salamis in the past, but what excited me most were the two huge metal grilling racks with neat little legs that would raise them above a bed of glowing gray and white embers, raked out from the fire behind. A method of cooking almost older than time, now mastered by the Tuscans. On the hearth at either side, were positioned two ancient and well-worn upturned logs—perfect seats for a warm-up on a cold, wet night. They also became the kitchen visitor's seats, where friends could sit and chat and view the comings and goings without being trodden underfoot by the cooks. I couldn't wait to get going, especially when I discovered a traditional domed brick bread oven behind a small black iron door

in the corner of the kitchen. It hadn't been used for years, and I decided there and then to incorporate it into my lessons. This lofty, warm kitchen was soon filled with the sounds of a crackling fire burning brightly to create enough embers to grill meaty sausages and spatchcocked quail and chicken. Aromas of olive oil, garlic, sage, and rosemary permeated the corridors leading from the kitchen, luring passers-by to come in and watch, chat, and taste. Bread and pizza dough would perch on the log stools to rise before being launched into the suffocating heat of the bread oven. It was in this kitchen that I held my first cooking classes and cooked countless evening meals. This was cooking heaven—especially when lit by candlelight during a storm-induced power-cut. We had fire and we could carry on cooking, and when you left the kitchen, the smell of wood smoke clung to your clothes—an evocative and comforting smell that I would catch a whiff of on my return home when opening my suitcase to unpack.

The third kitchen I worked in couldn't be more different. This was a kitchen built for cooking in the intense heat of the South. In fact, it was really two kitchens—one indoors opening out onto an almost Arabic, high-walled courtyard with a huge marble dining table and an open-air but covered kitchen beyond. Inside we cooked on gas and outside on a large brick barbecue, fuelled by wood charcoal. Food preparation was done inside to be out of the scorching sun in the small marble-floored kitchen. This being Sicily, all work surfaces were pale marble, cool, and easy to clean which was very important when dealing with abundant fish. Sensibly, all frying, broiling, and roasting was done in the outside kitchen, so that heat and smells were instantly dispelled. Dishes were finished off in the indoor kitchen behind its thick walls and shuttered windows. Cooking demonstrations would take place around the outdoor marble table and I could build up a nice tan while working at the same time—perfect! What a treat it was to work, teach, and eat in the open air under an insanely blue sky, shaded by two of the tallest palm trees I have ever seen. Enjoying glorious food and wine under a blue-black sky spangled with stars every night was breathtaking.

With good ingredients, a little basic cooking knowledge, and a big warm cook's heart, you are ready to cook Italian food. In this book I demonstrate the simple techniques used to create delicious regional dishes through recipes gathered from my travels in Italy. Where a description alone of the technique doesn't work, there are step-by-step illustrations, coupled with tips gleaned from working with wonderful Italian chefs from every corner of Italy. All the chefs I have worked with over the years have willingly shared with me their bountiful knowledge which I, in turn, now wish to share with you.

Italian cooking techniques are simple, because good natural ingredients need nothing much done to them to create great food. Cook with care and attention to the recipe, the taste and texture of the dish. Taste, taste, taste, and use your nose—if you don't taste a dish from beginning to end, you can't monitor the changes that take place during cooking. Start using your nose too and you will identify how to tell if a dish is ready just by smell alone. But, above all, don't be scared of using your hands—you have to feel food to understand it—and hands were there long before spoons! Have confidence in yourself and your cooking and this will show in the finished dish—much of the joy of cooking is in the preparation and in the reward of a dish that you have created yourself—no matter how simple. I hope this book serves as inspiration and helps to guide you through such techniques as soup-making, bread and pasta-making, grilling, and roasting to perfection, risotto-making, gnocchi rolling, and more. Great ingredients don't bite—buy the best you can afford, treat them with respect, and cook from your heart, and you will start to cook like an Italian.

antipasti

bruschetta

The word bruschetta is pronounced *broosketta* NOT *brooshetta*. The word may come from bruciare—the Italian word meaning to burn, and it is said to have originated in Lazio or Abruzzo. A satisfying rustic snack made with the simplest of ingredients to satisfy a hunger pang. Toasted bread like this was often placed in the bottom of a soup bowl with the soup poured on top to make a more satisfying meal. Whatever their size or shape, all these snacks should be freshly made with the best ingredients to hand—there's simply no excuse for a soggy bruschetta (or an overcooked, rock-hard one!).

traditional peasant tomato and garlic bruschetta
fettunta

4 large very ripe tomatoes

4 thick slices country bread, preferably sourdough

2 garlic cloves, halved

extra virgin olive oil, for sprinkling

sea salt and freshly ground black pepper

Serves 4

The word fettunta comes from the Tuscan dialect and derives from Latin, meaning "anointed slice." It is a slice of bread grilled over hot coals, rubbed with garlic, and sprinkled with olive oil. To be authentic you should use only the finest Tuscan extra virgin olive oil. The ripe tomato is just crushed in your hand and smashed onto the bread, then eaten immediately. This is bruschetta at its simplest and best. This is a more civilized version, but you should try the real thing—it's great fun! Use only the best and freshest ingredients for this.

Roughly chop the tomatoes and season with salt and pepper.

To make the bruschetta, grill, toast, or pan-grill the bread on both sides, until lightly browned or toasted. Rub the top side of each slice with the cut garlic, then sprinkle with olive oil.

Spoon the tomatoes over the bruschetta and sprinkle with more olive oil. Eat immediately with your fingers!

crostini

Crostini are smaller and more refined than bruschetta and make great vehicles for just about any combination of ingredients so let your imagination run riot! They are most often baked in the oven or fried until crisp but they do vary from region to region—in Tuscany, only one side is toasted, the topping being spread on the untoasted side. In the Veneto, crostini bases are crunchily fried or broiled golden polenta, making a very filling mouthful indeed displaying an interesting contrast of textures—crisp on the outside, but soft on the inside. Crostini are usually elegantly served with aperitivi and appear as a matter of course in Italian bars. Crostoni are just larger crostini.

1 Italian sfilatino or thin French baguette

extra virgin olive oil, for brushing

chopped flat-leaf parsley, to serve

tapénade:

6 oz oven-dried (Greek-style) black olives, pitted, about 1½ cups

2 garlic cloves

3 canned anchovies, drained

2 teaspoons capers, drained

1 tablespoon olive oil

white bean purée:

2 tablespoons olive oil

2 garlic cloves, finely chopped

1 teaspoon very finely chopped rosemary

1 small fresh red chile, seeded and finely chopped

1 lb. canned cannellini beans, rinsed and drained, about 1½ cups

sea salt and freshly ground black pepper

Serves 6–8

white bean and black olive crostini
crostini ai fagioli e tapénade

Here, the combination of bland creamy beans and sharp, rich, salty tapenade makes a sublime mouthful. You can use any type of canned bean for this, but the whiter they are the prettier they look. If you like, chop up some more black olives and sprinkle them on the bean purée or crumble some crisply cooked bacon over the top for extra crunch.

To make the crostini, preheat the oven to 375°F. Slice the bread into thin rounds, brush on both sides with olive oil and spread out on a baking sheet. Bake in the preheated oven for about 10 minutes, until lightly golden and crisp.

Put all the ingredients for the tapénade into a food processor and blend until smooth.

To make the bean purée, heat the oil in a small skillet and add the garlic. Cook gently for 2 minutes until golden but on no account brown. Stir in the rosemary and chile. Remove from the heat and add the beans with 3 tablespoons water. Mash the beans roughly in the pan and return to the heat until heated through. Season to taste with salt and pepper. Spread the crostini with tapénade and then add a spoonful of bean purée. Scatter with the chopped parsley and serve while warm.

pear, pecorino, and pea crostini
crostini alle pere, pecorino e piselli

1 Italian sfilatino or thin French baguette

extra virgin olive oil, for brushing and moistening

2 cups shelled fresh or frozen peas, about 8 oz.

freshly grated nutmeg

1 small ripe pear

a drop of balsamic or sherry vinegar or *vincotto ai fichi*

1 cup fresh young Pecorino or Parmesan cheese, diced, about 4 oz.

sea salt and freshly ground black pepper

Serves 6

An uplifting combination of fresh spring flavors and colors, and one of my favorites. Puréeing the peas gives a sweet, earthy base on which to sprinkle the combination of salty nutty Pecorino (Parmesan would work very well here too) and the fruitiness of pears tossed in a few drops of balsamic vinegar for sharpness, or to be even more fruity try to find *vincotto ai fichi* (a deliciously concentrated condiment of grape must, wine vinegar, and figs).

To make the crostini, preheat the oven to 375°F.

Slice the bread into thin rounds, brush on both sides with olive oil, and spread out on a baking sheet. Bake in the preheated oven for about 10 minutes, until lightly golden and crisp.

Meanwhile, blanch the peas in boiling water for 3 minutes if they are fresh or 2 minutes if they are frozen. Drain them, refresh in cold water, and drain again. Purée the peas in a food processor or blender, moistening with a little olive oil. Season with salt, pepper, and freshly grated nutmeg.

Core and finely chop the pear. Mix with a drop of balsamic vinegar, then add the cheese and mix well. Spread the crostini with a mound of pea purée and top with a spoonful of the pear and cheese mixture. Serve immediately.

zucchini and mint fritters
frittelle di zucchini e menta

This is my favorite way with zucchini! It changes their watery blandness into sweet and crunchy mouthfuls with just a hint of mint. Salting the zucchini before adding them to the batter draws out the water, concentrating the flavor. The batter is very light and, if fried at the correct temperature, it doesn't absorb any oil at all.

1¼ lb. zucchini
finely grated peel of 1 lemon
2 tablespoons freshly chopped mint
light olive oil, for frying
sea salt and freshly
ground black pepper
lemon wedges, to serve

batter:
2 eggs, separated
2 tablespoons olive oil
1 cup lager-style beer
1 cup all-purpose flour
sea salt and freshly
ground black pepper

an electric deep-fryer (optional)

Serves 4

To make the batter, put the egg yolks in a bowl, beat well, then slowly beat in the olive oil, followed by the beer, then the flour. Season with salt and pepper to taste. Cover and let rest for 1 hour.

Meanwhile, grate the zucchini coarsely, toss with salt, put in a strainer and let drain for 10 minutes. Rinse them well, then pat dry with paper towels. Put them in a bowl, add the lemon peel, mint, salt and pepper and stir well.

Just before cooking, put the egg whites, salt and pepper in a bowl and beat until firm. Gently fold into the batter. Heat the light olive oil to 375°F in a deep-fryer or a large saucepan with a frying basket. Mix the grated zucchini with just enough batter to bind them.

Working in batches, slide about 6 small spoonfuls of the battered zucchini at a time into the hot oil and fry for 2–3 minutes, until golden and crisp. Drain the fritters on paper towels, sprinkle with salt, and serve hot with lemon wedges.

choosing zucchini

Buy zucchini when the skins are taught and shiny—a zucchini should snap if bent—if not, and it just bends, then you have a sad, tired zucchini. Choose smaller zucchini as they contain less water and have more flavor. Don't worry about scratches and blemishes on the skin—it is thin and damages easily. Italians prefer them at their best, picked from the fields in summer.

However, if the zucchini in the bottom of your refrigerator drawer have seen better days—don't throw them out, all is not lost! Take a large bowl and fill with cold water, add a good handful of salt, and add your sliced or grated zucchini. Leave to soak in the refrigerator for 1 hour and the flagging vegetables will have perked up. Drain them through a colander, rinse in cold water, and pat dry as before.

Good Italian varieties to try include *Striata di Italia*, cream speckles, or stripes on a mid-green background is the favorite in Italy; *Tonda di Nizza*, brilliant dark green and round—for stuffing; *Verde di Milano*, the usual green one; *Bianca di Trieste* or *Sarda* are very pale green and sweet. There are many, many more.

spinach and ricotta timbales with sun-dried tomatoes, olives, capers, and herbs
timballi di ricotta, spinaci e condimenti

10 sun-dried (or sun-blushed) tomatoes in oil, drained

8 oz. fresh leaf spinach

1 lb. fresh ricotta cheese, well-drained

3 large eggs, beaten

12 oven-dried (Greek-style) black olives, pitted and chopped

2 tablespoons freshly chopped basil or oregano

2 tablespoons salted capers, rinsed and chopped, plus extra whole capers to serve

freshly grated nutmeg

sea salt and freshly ground black pepper

olive oil or fresh tomato sauce, to serve

6 dariole molds or ½-cup ramekins, generously buttered

Serves 6

These are little savory cheesecake towers, served warm with a sprinkle of olive oil or a small spoonful of a very rich tomato sauce. I always strain the ricotta for this, as it makes the mixture lighter. Beat the eggs into the cheese very well for even more lightness, and watch out for seasoning, as the capers and olives are quite salty. The bay leaf is crucial to the flavor here, and fresh leaves impart an almost nutmeg-like fragrance.

Preheat the oven to 375°F.

Put a sun-dried tomato in the bottom of each mold or ramekin. Thinly slice the remaining sun-dried tomatoes.

To prepare the spinach, remove the tough stems from the leaves, then wash the leaves really well and put them in a saucepan while still wet. Cook until the leaves wilt, then plunge into cold water. Drain very well and squeeze to extract any excess moisture. Loosen the leaves slightly.

Push the ricotta through a strainer or fine-mesh sieve or food mill to make it fluffy, then beat in the eggs. Lightly stir in the drained, wilted spinach, sliced sun-dried tomatoes, olives, basil, and capers. Season to taste with salt, pepper, and nutmeg. Spoon the ricotta mixture into the prepared molds and level, then put on a baking sheet.

Bake in the preheated oven for 20 minutes, until almost set and a little puffed. Remove from the oven and let cool slightly. Turn out onto small plates, then serve at room temperature with extra capers and a sprinkle of olive oil or a spoonful of fresh tomato sauce.

1

2

fresh tuna carpaccio
carpaccio di tonno

8-oz. piece of sashimi-grade tuna or swordfish or swordfish loin (thin end)

about 1 cup arugula

freshly shaved Parmesan cheese

dressing:

freshly squeezed juice of 3 lemons

⅔ cup extra virgin olive oil

1 garlic clove, finely chopped

1 tablespoon salted capers, rinsed and chopped

a pinch of hot red pepper flakes

sea salt and freshly ground black pepper

Serves 4

One of the finest sights in a southern Italian fish market is a whole tuna fish being deftly portioned by men wielding the sharpest of cleavers, singing and shouting to come and buy their magnificent catch. You can be sure it is spanking fresh, and it is perfect for making *carpaccio*—the Italian equivalent of sashimi. Chilling or lightly freezing it makes it firm enough to slice very thinly. As soon as the slices hit plates at room temperature, they become meltingly soft. I have also seen smoked salmon and smoked swordfish served this way in Italy.

Trim the tuna of any membrane or gristle. Wrap tightly in plastic wrap and freeze for about 1 hour, until just frozen but not rock solid.

Meanwhile, to make the dressing, put the lemon juice, olive oil, garlic, capers, pepper flakes, salt, and pepper in a bowl and beat until emulsified.

Unwrap the tuna, slice it thinly with a sharp, thin-bladed knife. If this proves difficult, an easier way is to cut slices from the tuna and lay them between two sheets of plastic wrap.

(1) Bat out gently with a rolling pin, taking care not to make holes in the tuna.

(2) Finish off by gently rolling the tuna out to the desired thickness—this will remove any ridges left by batting it out.

Arrange the slices so they completely cover 4 large dinner plates. Spoon the dressing over the top. Add a tangle of arugula and sprinkle with Parmesan shavings, then serve.

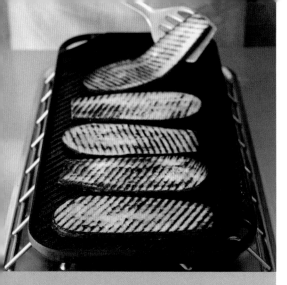

three marinated antipasti
tre antipasti marinati

The best antipasti are an appealing mix of colors, flavors, and textures, to whet the palate before the meal ahead. Marinating these morsels for at least 2 hours before serving gives them extra savor. Serve all three together on a large platter for maximum impact. The platter will serve four people.

grilling vegetables

This method of grilling extracts and concentrates the sweetness of most vegetables. Contact with the direct heat of a ridged grill pan turns the naturally occurring sugars in the vegetable juices to caramel, and it is this caramel that adds the delicious smoky flavor. Your grill pan should be made of cast iron and very heavy. This ensures even cooking as the pan will distribute the heat evenly, unlike a lightweight pan. The more finely cut the vegetable, the quicker it will cook but it will burn and disintegrate if you don't watch it like a hawk.

Heat the pan over a medium-high heat until it is smoking. Only cook as many vegetable slices as the pan will hold. Overcrowding the pan will spoil the effect and taste. Brush the vegetables lightly with olive or sunflower oil, but not the grill pan. Oiling the pan just produces acrid smoke! Watch the vegetables carefully and lift the edges up with a spatula from time to time to check the color. When they are nicely striped on the first side, turn them over and cook until that side is striped, and the vegetables are cooked through. Season with salt and freshly ground black pepper as soon as they come off the pan.

grilled bell pepper, mozzarella, and pesto roulades
involtini di peperoni, mozzarella e pesto

2 large red bell peppers

6 oz. fresh mozzarella

8 large basil leaves

1 tablespoon Classic Pesto Genovese (page 71)

extra virgin olive oil

sea salt and freshly ground black pepper

Grill or broil the bell peppers until soft and black. Rinse off the skins, cut the peppers in quarters lengthwise, cut off the stalks and scrape out the seeds. Cut the mozzarella into 8 thin slices. Put a slice inside each pepper strip, put a basil leaf on top, and season well with salt and pepper. Roll up from one end and secure with a toothpick. Put the pesto in a bowl and beat in enough olive oil to thin it to pouring consistency. Add the rolls and toss to coat. Cover and let marinate before serving.

grilled eggplant with salami and artichoke
melanzane alla griglia con salame e carciofi

1 medium eggplant

⅓ cup olive oil, plus extra for brushing

8 thin slices salami

4 artichokes marinated in oil, drained and halved

2 tablespoons freshly squeezed lemon juice

1 tablespoon capers, rinsed, drained, and chopped

sea salt and freshly ground black pepper

Heat a ridged grill pan until hot (see box left). Cut the eggplant into 8 thin slices, brush lightly with olive oil and cook for 2–3 minutes on each side. Put a slice of salami on each one, then a halved artichoke at one side. Fold the eggplant in half to cover the artichoke, secure with a toothpick and put in a shallow, non-reactive dish. Put the ⅓ cup olive oil in a bowl, beat in the lemon juice, capers, salt and pepper, then spoon over the eggplant. Cover and let marinate before serving.

grilled zucchini marinated in lemon
zucchine alla griglia marinate al limone

3 zucchini

¼ cup olive oil, plus extra for brushing

2 tablespoons freshly squeezed lemon juice

1 tablespoon freshly grated Parmesan cheese

2 anchovy fillets, rinsed and finely chopped

toothpicks
a ridged grill pan

Cut the zucchini into long thin slices, brush with olive oil and cook on the same grill pan for 2–3 minutes on each side. Transfer to a shallow, non-reactive dish. Put the 4 tablespoons olive oil, lemon juice, Parmesan, and anchovies in a bowl, beat with a fork, then pour over the zucchini. Cover and let marinate before serving.

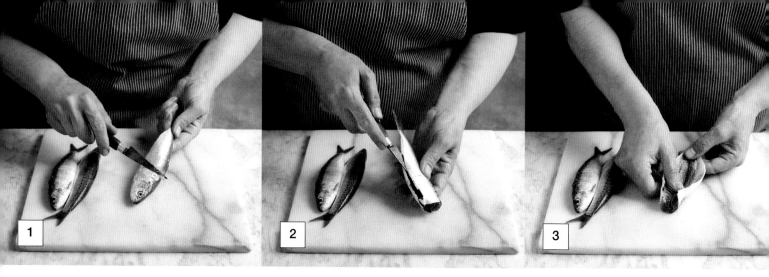

fresh anchovies marinated in lemon and chile
acciughe al limone e peperoncino

16 fresh anchovies or small sardines

freshly squeezed juice of 2 lemons

1 small dried red chile, seeded and finely chopped

2 large scallions, thinly sliced

2 tablespoons freshly chopped flat-leaf parsley

extra virgin olive oil, for sprinkling

sea salt and freshly ground black pepper

Serves 4

There's nothing quite like a dish of these light-tasting, fresh, silvery morsels eaten fillet by fillet with a chilled glass of *vino bianco*. If you've never tried a fresh anchovy before and see some in a market, buy them! They have a mild flavor, not at all like the canned fillets in oil. Fresh anchovies like these are even found on the glorious fish counters of larger supermarkets in Italy. You can, however, substitute very small sardines.

(1) Remove the scales from the fish by holding the tail and gently scraping the back of a knife along the body from the tail to the head. The scales will ping off! Be careful not to press too hard or you will damage the delicate flesh. Turn the fish over and repeat with the other side. Rinse well.

(2) Cut off the heads just behind the gills and slit open the soft bellies (using a knife or scissors). Pull out the small amount of guts and rinse the cavity.

(3) Slide your thumb along the backbone to release the flesh along its length.

(4) Take hold of the backbone from the head end and lift it out, easing it away from the flesh. Try to keep the tails on for presentation.

(5) Place the fillets skin-side up in a shallow non-reactive dish and pour over the freshly squeezed lemon juice. Scatter with chile, gently lift the fillets by the tails to mix them with the juice and chile. Cover and marinate in the refrigerator for 24 hours.

The next day, lift the fillets out of the juice (they will look pale and "cooked") and lay them on a serving dish. Sprinkle them with the scallions and parsley, and liberally anoint with olive oil. Season with salt and pepper and serve at room temperature.

Cook's note: If your lemons are very sharp, add a small pinch of sugar to the freshly squeezed juice.

deep-fried sage leaves
salvia fritta

24 large sage leaves
1 teaspoon salted capers, rinsed
1 tablespoon anchovy paste
vegetable oil, for deep-frying

batter:
1 egg
⅔ cup ice water
1 cup all-purpose flour

Makes 12

This may seem like a mad thing to do, but try it—the explosion of flavors when you bite into the light, crunchy morsels, is out of this world. I sometimes cheat and use a packet of Japanese tempura batter—quick, easy, and fail-me-never! Serve these straight out of the pan to preserve their crispness.

Wash and dry the sage leaves. Mash the capers with the anchovy paste and spread onto the darker green sides of 12 of the leaves. Press another leaf on top of the filling to form a sandwich.

To make the batter, lightly beat the egg and the ice water together. Add the flour and beat again, leaving the mixture a bit lumpy. Do not allow to stand.

Heat the vegetable oil in a deep pan or wok until a piece of stale bread turns golden in a few seconds when dropped in. Holding the sage leaves by the stem, carefully dip them into the batter and lightly shake off the excess. Place into the hot oil, a few at a time, and fry until crisp and barely golden. This will only take a few seconds. Drain on paper towels and serve immediately while still warm.

salads and vegetables
insalate e contorni

artichokes
carciofi

There are more than 90 varieties worldwide of this delicious "edible thistle" and Italy is the top producer. They range from tiny and spiny to tightly oval, purply green beauties to big, round, and blousy globes. In general, the ones with vicious spines tend to come from the parched hot climate of the south and are quite dangerous to prepare, and the more familiar globe artichokes are from the cooler climes. If cut in half from stem to tip you will see spines on the tips of the tough outer "leaves" (but not always), layers of leaves showing thicker and greener to the outside, becoming thinner and pale yellow sometimes tinged with purple towards the inside. Working up from the stem—which is edible if peeled—you have the artichoke base or *fondo*—the ultimate delicacy. On top of the base is the furry "choke" which is edible in young artichokes, but should be removed from larger mature specimens. Artichoke hearts are the bases with some of the tender leaves still attached. To see beautifully prepared artichokes, visit The Rialto Market in Venice in March and April—it's artichoke heaven!

Preparing small oval artichokes with long stems (such as *Violetto di Toscana*)

Fill a large bowl with cold water and add lemon halves, squeezing in the juice to acidulate it. Have a couple of halved lemons on the side to rub the cut portions of each artichoke as you work.

(1) Pull off and discard any large leaves from the stem. (2) Trim the stalk down to about 2 inches.

(3) Holding the stem and starting at the base, snap off the tough dark green/purple outer leaves right at the base until you are left with only the pale interior leaves.

(4) Trim and neaten the dark green outer layer around the base and using a vegetable peeler or sharp knife, peel off the fiberous outside of the stalk.

(5) Rub the exposed cut flesh with a lemon half to lessen the discoloration. (6) Cut about ½ inch off the tip of each artichoke.

Place each artichoke in the acidulated water until needed to stop them discoloring. Do not soak for longer than 2 hours. They are ready to be boiled or fried in olive oil or as your recipe dictates.

Cook's note: You may like to wear thin disposable gloves to prevent your hands from staining!

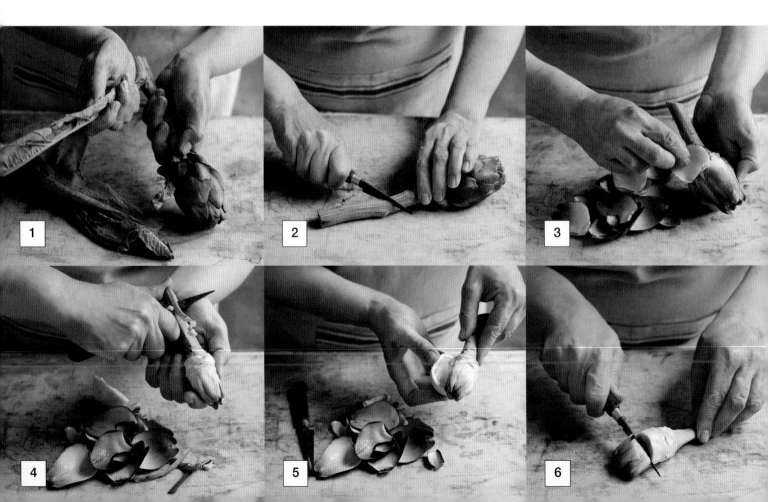

Preparing larger globe artichokes (such as *Romanesco* and *Precoce di Chioggia*)

First prepare a large bowl of cold acidulated water (see method left).

(1) Starting at the base, snap off the thick stem—this should pull out some of the tough fibers with it. Snap off any really tough and discolored leaves.

(2) Using scissors, snip off the tough tips of the remaining leaves.

(3) Neaten the base so that it will sit up straight.

(4) Put the artichokes into the bowl of acidulated cold water as you go.

(5) Transfer the artichokes to a large pot of simmering, salted water and cover with a sheet of baking parchment. Cook for about 20 minutes, or until the bases are tender when tested with a sharp knife—there should be no resistance.

(6) Carefully lift out the artichokes and turn upside-down to drain. Turn them the right way up again, gently tease open the top to reveal the pale yellow leaves and pull these out.

(7) Once these leaves are removed they reveal the hairy choke. Carefully scoop out the choke with a spoon.

(8) Gently close up the artichoke again. It is now ready to eat with melted butter, olive oil, or mayonnaise for dipping the leaves into.

To eat, pull off the outer leaves starting at the base and dip in the sauce, then bite off the soft part found at the base each leaf. Discard the tough leaves in a pile as you go. When all the leaves are gone—the *fondo* remains. Eat this with a knife and fork, dipping as you go.

spinach with eggs
spinaci con uovi

My version of the famous dish of baked eggs nestling on a bed of spinach and *salsa besciamella*, uses cream to lighten the whole effect and enhance the delicate flavors.

2 lb. fresh leaf spinach
3 tablespoons salted butter
1 cup light cream
4 eggs
freshly grated nutmeg
3 tablespoons freshly grated Parmesan cheese
sea salt and freshly ground black pepper

Serves 4

Preheat the oven to 400°F. Pull the stalks off the spinach, wash the leaves very well in plenty of cold water, then chop roughly. Melt the butter in a large pan, add the spinach and cook until wilted. Lift out the spinach and drain through a colander, catching any juices that run out.

Arrange the spinach in a buttered baking dish. Pour over the cream, then make 4 indentations in the spinach and crack an egg into each one. Pour the spinach juices back into the pan and boil to reduce. Season with salt, pepper, and grated nutmeg and pour into the dish. Sprinkle with Parmesan and bake in the preheated oven for about 15–20 minutes, or until the eggs are set and the dish is bubbling.

peas with prosciutto
piselli al prosciutto

Fresh peas need almost no cooking at all, and this dish makes the most of their freshness. If I have time, I like to make use of the pea pods which are bursting with flavor, so I make a quick pea stock to give the dish extra flavor. Add more stock if the dish looks dry—there should be plenty of sweet, buttery juices.

2 lb. fresh peas in their pods (to give about ½ lb. shelled weight)
5 oz. prosciutto, or any thickly sliced Italian ham
3 tablespoons butter
1 small onion, finely chopped
sea salt and freshly ground black pepper

Serves 4

Open the pea pods and remove the peas with your thumb, reserving the pods and peas separately. Roughly chop the pods, put them into a saucepan, barely cover with water and bring to a boil. Simmer for 10 minutes, strain and set aside.

Slice the prosciutto into thin strips. Melt the butter in a medium saucepan, add the onion, and cook gently for 5 minutes until softening but not coloring. Add the fresh peas and ½ cup pea stock, and salt and pepper to taste. Stir well, then cover and simmer for 5 minutes. Uncover and stir in the prosciutto. Cook over a medium heat for a couple of minutes, then serve immediately.

baked tomatoes with basil and melting mozzarella
fonduta di pomodori

In Italy, the best mozzarella is made from water buffalo milk and is a delicacy ideally enjoyed fresh as can be and on its own with just a drizzle of best extra virgin olive oil. The majority sold is made from cow's milk (*fior di latte* being the best of the commercially made stuff) and comes in fist-size balls, small plaits or *bocconcini* (little bite-size balls). The delicate lactic flavor of *mozzarella di bufala* would be lost here and is best kept for salads. Use balls of regular mozzarella or *bocconcini*, which would be perfect for this dish, although they are more expensive than the larger balls.

12 medium tomatoes (about 2 lb.)
extra virgin olive oil, for drizzling
1 cup basil leaves, finely sliced
8 oz. mozzarella cheese, diced
or about 25 *bocconcini*
sea salt and freshly
ground black pepper

Serves 4

Preheat the oven to 350°F.

Cut the tomatoes in half around their "equators" and arrange them cut-side up in an oiled baking dish. Make sure they are packed together tightly in a single layer, because you want them to collapse into a solid layer of gooey tomato when cooked.

Sprinkle with salt, grind over plenty of black pepper, and drizzle with lots of olive oil.

Bake in the preheated oven for about 1 hour. If they have not collapsed and concentrated by this time, cook for longer. When cooked, remove from the oven, put the basil on the tomatoes, then scatter the mozzarella on top of the basil.

Return to the cooling oven for 2 minutes to help the mozzarella melt—on no account should it brown, just let it melt into creamy pools. Serve immediately.

baking tomatoes

It's possible to transform even the dullest supermarket tomatoes into a Mediterranean delight!

Baking the tomatoes as I've done here in this recipe, reduces them to the "mi-cuit" or "half-cooked" stage. In other words, all the water in the tomato halves evaporates slowly and concentrates the flavor without the tomatoes losing any of their juiciness. Tomatoes cooked in this way are more moist than the more familiar semi-dried or oven-dried tomatoes which are prepared in exactly the same way, but cooked for longer (about 2 hours) until much firmer.

The tomatoes should always be arranged cut-side uppermost so that the moisture can escape easily, and packed together tightly in a single layer to ensure that they don't dry out during the long cooking time needed to really concentrate their flavor.

Adding *aromi* like a sprinkling of dried oregano, chopped garlic, or a grinding of sea salt and black pepper, adds to the concentrated sweetness.

grilled eggplant with lemon, mint, and balsamic vinegar
melanzane alla griglia con salsa di menta

2 medium eggplants (about 14 oz.)

olive oil, for basting

dressing:

½ cup extra virgin olive oil

finely grated peel and freshly squeezed juice of 1 lemon

2 tablespoons balsamic vinegar

1–2 teaspoons sugar

¼ cup very coarsely chopped mint

sea salt and freshly ground black pepper

a ridged grill pan or barbecue

Serves 4

Although simplicity itself to make, the success of this dish relies on grilling the eggplants perfectly (see my guide on page 22). There is nothing worse than an undercooked eggplant, so make sure you baste with plenty of oil, and don't let the pan get too hot or the eggplants will burn before they brown—they should gently sizzle. Add a little crushed or chopped garlic to the dressing if you like, but the mint and lemon flavors are quite delicate so show restraint.

To make the dressing, put the oil, lemon peel and juice, and balsamic vinegar in a bowl and beat well. Add the sugar, salt, and pepper to taste—it should be fairly sweet. Stir in half the mint, then set aside.

Heat a ridged grill pan until hot or light a barbecue and wait for the coals to turn white. Cut each eggplant lengthwise into 8 thin slices, brush liberally with olive oil, add to the pan or barbecue, and cook for 2–3 minutes on each side, until golden brown and lightly charred. Arrange the slices on a large platter and spoon the dressing over the top.

Cover and set aside so that the eggplant absorbs the flavors of the dressing. Sprinkle with the remaining chopped mint and serve warm or at room temperature.

sicilian sweet and sour eggplant stew
caponata

This stalwart of the Sicilian menu when made well tastes like a rich and exotic "ratatouille." It originates from coastal bars (*caupone* in Sicilian) frequented by fishermen. It contained soaked dried ship's biscuit to satisfy appetites after days of deprivation at sea, but thankfully the biscuit has now disappeared! It tastes better the next day, so store in the refrigerator but serve at room temperature.

4 medium eggplants,
cut into bite-size cubes

¼ cup olive oil

1 onion, chopped

2 celery ribs, sliced

12 very ripe large tomatoes, coarsely chopped, or 28 oz. canned chopped tomatoes

1–2 tablespoons salted capers, rinsed well

½ cup best green olives, stoned

2 tablespoons red wine vinegar

2 teaspoons sugar

sea salt

vegetable oil, for frying

to serve:
about 8 oz. fresh ricotta cheese
chopped toasted almonds
freshly chopped flat-leaf parsley

an electric deep-fryer (optional)

Serves 6

Put the eggplants in a colander and salt them (see left).

Heat the olive oil in a saucepan and add the onion and celery. Cook for 5 minutes until softened but not browned, add the tomatoes, then cook for 15 minutes until pulpy. Add the capers, olives, vinegar, and sugar to the sauce and cook for a further 15 minutes.

Meanwhile, heat the vegetable oil to 375°F in a deep-fryer. Add the salted eggplant cubes in batches and fry until deep golden brown. This may take some time, but cook them thoroughly, because undercooked eggplant is unpleasant. Alternatively, toss the cubes in olive oil, spread them out in a roasting pan and roast in an oven preheated to 400°F for 20 minutes, or until well browned and tender.

Stir the eggplants into the tomato sauce. Taste and adjust the seasoning (this means adding more sugar or vinegar to taste to balance the flavors). Set aside for at least 30 minutes or overnight to develop the flavors before serving. Serve warm or at room temperature in a shallow bowl and top with the ricotta, almonds, and parsley.

salting eggplants

I learned this trick many years ago. It does make salting eggplants very easy. The reason for salting is that the spongy flesh tends to absorb less oil when cooking. One thing I would urge though is don't skimp on the oil when cooking eggplant—it needs it to help draw the heat into the flesh to cook it and keeps it moist. If too little oil is used when grilling or frying, the eggplant will be tasteless and dry.

To salt, dissolve a handful of salt in a large bowl of cold water and add the sliced or diced eggplant to it. Set a lid or plate on top to keep them submerged and leave for about 1 hour to draw out the bitter juices. After this time, tip into a colander, rinse, and pat dry with paper towels. You can then use the eggplant as directed in your recipe.

When frying, roasting, or broiling, make sure the eggplant is well-colored for maximum flavor but not burnt— it will taste bitter and unpleasant.

cannellini beans with olive oil and mint
fagioli bianchi in umido con la menta

2½ cups dried cannellini, haricot,
or navy beans

2 garlic cloves, unpeeled but smashed open

6–8 mint leaves, plus 3 tablespoons freshly
chopped or torn mint

⅓ cup extra virgin olive oil

1 small red onion, thinly sliced into rings,
or half moons

sea salt and freshly ground black pepper

Serves 4

Any type of dried bean will work well in this recipe—only the cooking times will differ. To make sure that the onion isn't too strong, soak the slices in cold water for 10 minutes and this will draw out the strong juice. Alternatively, you could blanch them for 1 minute in boiling water, to which a couple of squeezes of lemon juice have been added—this will soften the texture and flavor.

Soak the beans overnight in three times their volume of cold water.

The next day, drain and put them in a large saucepan. Add the garlic cloves, the whole mint leaves, and pepper. Cover with cold water, slowly bring to a boil, then turn down the heat and simmer for 25–30 minutes, until tender. Times will vary according to the age of the beans. Drain well and remove the garlic and mint.

Put the olive oil, chopped mint, and onion in a bowl and mix with a fork. Add the drained beans and toss them carefully with the dressing. Taste and check the seasoning—you may have to add a little salt—and serve warm or at room temperature.

warm lentil, mushroom, tomato, and arugula salad
insalata di lenticchie, porcini, pomodori e rucola

1 cup green or brown lentils

1 small onion, cut in half

1 carrot, cut in half

1 celery rib, cut in half

1 bay leaf

3 garlic cloves, 2 lightly crushed but kept whole and 1 finely chopped

⅔ cup extra virgin olive oil, plus about 1 tablespoon for frying

4 oz. pancetta (Italian bacon), cut into matchsticks

1 lb. large flat mushrooms or fresh porcini, wiped and thickly sliced

3 tablespoons red wine vinegar

½ teaspoon sugar

12 sun-blushed tomatoes, cut in half

6 scallions, white and green parts, chopped

10 oz. arugula

sea salt and freshly ground black pepper

Serves 6

Don't be deceived by the "vegetarian" title of this recipe—it is rich and filling and bursting with flavor, and is one of my most popular starters on my cooking holidays. It tastes even better if you make it with a mix of dried wild and fresh mushrooms, or even fresh shiitake mushrooms. The best lentils in Italy are said to come from Umbria. Make this salad with any tomato you like with the exception of sun-dried tomatoes—they are too dry.

Put the lentils, onion, carrot, celery, bay leaf, and crushed garlic cloves in a large saucepan. Add enough water to completely cover all the ingredients. Bring to a boil, then turn down the heat and simmer for about 45 minutes, or until the lentils are tender but not falling apart and mushy. Drain well. Remove and discard the vegetables, then transfer the lentils to a large serving bowl.

Heat about 1 tablespoon oil in a skillet, add the pancetta, and cook until golden and crisp. Remove the pancetta, drain on paper towels and add to the lentils. Return the pan to the heat and add the mushrooms. Fry for 2–3 minutes, then add to the lentils.

Add the chopped garlic to the hot pan, along with a little more oil if necessary, and fry until just beginning to color. Immediately add the vinegar, scraping up any sticky bits in the pan. Add the sugar and boil until it is dissolved. Stir in the olive oil and heat gently—do not let it boil. Season to taste with salt and pepper.

Add the tomatoes, scallions, and arugula to the lentils and mix well. Pour over the hot dressing and toss lightly but thoroughly. Serve immediately before the salad goes soggy.

grilled and sautéed mushrooms
funghi trifolati

4 large portobello mushrooms
or 4 large fresh porcini mushrooms

olive oil (see method)

1 cup white wine

2 garlic cloves, chopped

freshly squeezed juice of 1 lemon

3 tablespoons freshly chopped flat-leaf parsley

sea salt and freshly ground black pepper

a heavy grill pan

Serves 4

You will often see this on menus, and it usually means that the mushrooms are sliced and sautéed, then finished off with the reduction of wine and olive oil. This is good if the mushrooms are small, but when it is mushroom season and you have the opportunity of cooking larger mushrooms, then the method below is the way to do it. When big porcini mushroom caps are grilled over a bed of wood charcoal, the smell is fantastic! Complete the dish with a wine reduction and masses of chopped parsley.

Heat a heavy grill pan until hot or preheat the broiler to high. Pull the stalks off from the mushroom caps, chop the stalks finely, and set aside. Brush the caps with olive oil. Turn gill-side up, sprinkle with more olive oil, and season with salt and pepper. Set the mushroom caps, still gill-side up, on the hot grill pan and cook for 3 minutes or so, depending on size, then turn over and cook for a further 2 minutes. If broiling, place in the broiler pan, gill-side up, and broil for about 5 minutes, without turning, until tender.

Meanwhile, put 3 tablespoons olive oil in a skillet with the white wine, garlic, lemon juice, parsley, and the reserved chopped mushroom stalks. Bring to a boil, then boil hard to reduce by half. Season well and take off the heat.

Transfer the mushrooms to warm serving plates and pour or spoon the sauce over the top. Serve immediately.

soups
minestre

vegetable stock
brodo vegetale

1 large onion, quartered

2 large carrots, quartered

1 small bunch of celery, coarsely chopped (including leaves)

2 leeks, white parts only, cut in half lengthwise, rinsed, and cut in half again

4 zucchini, thickly sliced

2 tomatoes, cut in half around the middle and seeds squeezed out

1 fennel bulb, quartered

1 romaine lettuce heart, coarsely chopped

3 garlic cloves

1 dried red chile

4 fresh bay leaves

a handful of parsley stalks, crushed

½ lemon, sliced

6 black peppercorns

sea salt, to taste

a piece of cheesecloth for lining a colander (not needed if you have a fine strainer)

Makes 2–3 quarts

Too many vegetable stocks are insipid or taste of a single ingredient. This stock seems extravagant in its use of vegetables, but will have very good flavor. Stock gives a risotto body and depth of flavor, but shouldn't dominate the dish. Strong root vegetables such as rutabaga and parsnips are not good additions, and neither are potatoes or cabbage. Although you should always use the best and freshest ingredients, bits and pieces lurking in the refrigerator vegetable drawer can be used. Remember to wash everything first or you will end up with gritty stock. If you want a stronger stock, just strain, then boil hard to reduce it.

(1) Prepare the vegetables.

(2) Put all the ingredients into a large soup kettle, and cover with about 4 quarts cold water. Bring to a boil and simmer for 15 minutes.

(3) Stir the stock and skim, then cook at the barest simmer for 1 hour, skimming often.

(4) Remove from the heat and strain the stock into a bowl through a fine strainer or colander lined with cheesecloth. Discard the contents of the strainer after they have cooled. Cool the stock and refrigerate for several hours.

At this stage you can reboil the stock to concentrate it, or cover and chill in the refrigerator or freeze until needed.

The stock will keep in the refrigerator for 3 days or in the freezer for up to 6 months.

chicken stock
brodo di pollo

3½ lb. chicken wings

2 carrots, coarsely chopped

2 onions, coarsely chopped

1 whole small bunch of celery, including any leaves, trimmed, coarsely chopped, then washed

a few black peppercorns

bouquet garni:

4 fresh bay leaves

4 sprigs of thyme

2 sprigs of rosemary

6 parsley stalks, no leaves

a few celery leaves

kitchen string
a piece of cheesecloth for lining a colander

Makes 2–3 quarts

Although Italians are not shy of using bouillon cubes (*dadi da brodo*), a good stock is worth making and can add real depth of flavor to a soup. It is important not to make the stock too concentrated or dark in color—it mustn't mask the true flavors in the soup. You can make the stock by using a whole chicken instead of chicken wings if you like, but I think this is sometimes a waste and chicken wings are flavorsome and give a good jellied stock.

(1) To make the bouquet garni, bundle the bay leaves, thyme, rosemary, parsley stalks, and celery leaves together and tie securely with kitchen string. Set aside until needed.

(2) Cut the chicken wings into pieces through their joints. Put these into a large soup kettle with the carrots, onions, celery, and peppercorns.

(3) Add enough cold water to cover, about 4 quarts, and add the bouquet garni. Bring to a boil. As soon as it boils, reduce the heat to a simmer, stir, and skim.

(4) Continue to cook at the barest simmer for 3 hours, skimming often. Remove from the heat and strain the stock into a bowl through a colander lined with cheesecloth.

When cool, discard the contents of the colander. Cool the stock and refrigerate for several hours. Remove from the refrigerator and lift off any fat that has set on top of the jellied stock. At this stage you can reboil the stock to concentrate it, or cover and refrigerate or freeze until needed. This stock will keep in the refrigerator for 3–4 days or in the freezer for up to 6 months.

1

2

3

4

la ribollita

1 lb. dried cannellini beans

⅔ cup extra virgin olive oil

1 onion, finely chopped

1 carrot, chopped

1 celery rib, chopped

2 leeks, finely chopped

4 garlic cloves, finely chopped

1 small white (Dutch) cabbage, shredded

1 large potato, peeled and chopped

4 zucchini, chopped

2½ cups passata (Italian sieved tomatoes)

2 sprigs rosemary

2 sprigs thyme

2 sprigs sage

1 whole dried hot red pepper

2 lb. *cavolo nero* (Tuscan black winter cabbage) or savoy cabbage, finely shredded

sea salt and freshly ground black pepper

to serve:

6 thick slices coarse crusty white bread

1 garlic clove, peeled and bruised

extra virgin olive oil

freshly grated Parmesan cheese

Serves 8

I know I am truly back in Tuscany when I see *cavolo nero* (Tuscan black winter cabbage) growing in rows in small allotments, looking like mini palm trees. Savoy cabbage makes a good alternative here, however. This basic bean and vegetable soup is usually made one day, then reheated the next, when the flavors will have really developed. It is ladled over toasted garlic bread, drizzled with olive oil, and served with lots of Parmesan cheese. This is the perfect soup for a big family get-together, best made in quantity, and is very filling. *Ribollita* literally means "reboiled" and is made from whatever vegetables are around, but must contain beans, and the delicious *cavolo nero* or savoy cabbage.

Soak the cannellini beans overnight in plenty of cold water.

Heat half the olive oil in a soup kettle or heavy-based saucepan and add the onion, carrot, and celery. Cook gently for 10 minutes, stirring frequently. Add the leeks and garlic and cook for another 10 minutes. Add the white cabbage, potato, and zucchini, stir well and cook for 10 minutes, stirring frequently.

Stir in the soaked beans, passata, rosemary, thyme, sage, dried pepper, salt, and plenty of black pepper. Cover with about 2 quarts water (the vegetables should be well-covered), bring to a boil, then turn down the heat, and simmer, covered, for at least 2 hours, until the beans are very soft.

Transfer 2–3 large ladlefuls of soup to a bowl and mash well using the back of the ladle. Return to the soup to thicken it. Stir in the *cavolo nero* and simmer for another 15 minutes. Allow to cool, then refrigerate overnight.

The next day, slowly reheat the soup and stir in the remaining olive oil. Toast the bread and rub with garlic. Arrange the bread over the base of a tureen or warmed serving bowls and ladle the soup over it. Drizzle with extra olive oil and serve with plenty of Parmesan.

creamy tomato and bread soup with basil oil
pappa al pomodoro

6 cups vegetable or chicken stock (see pages 50–53), or beef stock

¼ cup extra virgin olive oil

1 onion, peeled and chopped

2½ lb. very ripe, soft tomatoes, chopped

10 oz. stale white bread, crusts removed and thinly sliced or made into bread crumbs

3 garlic cloves, peeled and crushed

2 cups Parmesan cheese, freshly grated, plus extra to serve

sea salt and freshly ground black pepper

basil and arugula oil:

⅔ cup extra virgin olive oil

3 tablespoons freshly chopped basil

3 tablespoons chopped arugula

Serves 6

Pappa al pomodoro is only as good as its ingredients—great tomatoes, good bread, and wonderful, green olive oil. This is one of the most comforting soups on earth and, as you might expect, has its origins in peasant thriftiness. Leftover bread is never thrown away in Tuscany as there is always a use for it. Here it thickens a rich tomato soup, which is in turn enriched with Parmesan—a nod to modern tastes as an aged local pecorino would traditionally have been used. You will see this soup on every menu around Florence, Siena, and Arezzo, but it is hard to find a good one. My addition is the flavored oil—in Tuscany you would be given extra virgin olive oil to pour over the soup.

Heat the stock slowly in a large saucepan. Meanwhile, heat the oil in a separate large saucepan, add the onion and tomatoes and fry over a gentle heat for 10 minutes until soft. Push the mixture through a food mill, mouli, or sieve, and stir into the stock. Add the bread and garlic. Cover and simmer gently for about 45 minutes, until thick and creamy, giving a good whisk every now and then to break up the bread. Watch out, as this soup can catch on the bottom of the pan.

To make the basil and arugula oil, process the olive oil, basil, and arugula in a food processor or blender until completely smooth, then pour through a fine strainer, if necessary. Stir the Parmesan into the soup and season to taste with salt and pepper. Ladle the soup into bowls, drizzle each serving with 2 tablespoons basil and arugula oil, and serve hot, warm or cold (but never chilled). Serve extra Parmesan separately.

venetian pea and rice soup with mint
risi e bisi alla menta

5 cups vegetable or chicken stock (see pages 50–53), or beef stock

2 tablespoons olive oil

4 tablespoons butter

2 oz. pancetta (Italian bacon), finely chopped

1 large scallion (*cipolloto*) or the white parts of 4 scallions, finely chopped

1 cup risotto rice, preferably *vialone nano*

2½ lb. fresh peas in the pod, shelled, or 1 lb. frozen peas

3 tablespoons freshly chopped mint

freshly grated Parmesan cheese, to serve

sea salt and freshly ground black pepper

Serves 4

A lovely soup to serve in the summer when fresh peas and mint are plentiful. *Vialone nano* is the favorite risotto rice in the Veneto region. It is a semi-fino round grain rice, best for soups and risotti, but *arborio* (a superfino used mainly for risotti) will do very nicely. This dish has very ancient roots and was flavored with fennel seeds at one time. Parsley is the usual addition now, but I prefer fresh mint in the summer months.

Put the stock in a large saucepan and bring it slowly to a boil while you prepare the *soffritto* (sautéed sauce).

Heat the oil and 2 tablespoons of the butter in a separate large saucepan and, when melted, add the pancetta and scallion. Cook for about 5 minutes, until softened but not browned.

Pour in the rice, stir for a few minutes to toast it, then add the hot stock. Simmer for about 10 minutes, stirring from time to time. Add the peas, cook for another 5–7 minutes, then stir in the remaining butter, mint, and Parmesan. The rice grains should not be too mushy, and the soup should be thick, but not stodgy.

Add salt and pepper to taste, ladle into warmed serving bowls and serve immediately.

pasta and bean soup
pasta e fagioli

1¼ cup dried cannellini or haricot beans

a pinch of baking soda

¼ cup olive oil, plus extra to serve

2 garlic cloves, crushed

1¾ quarts vegetable or chicken stock (see pages 50–53), or water

1 cup short pasta shapes, such as maccheroni or tubetti

4 tomatoes, peeled, seeded and coarsely chopped

¼ cup freshly chopped flat-leaf parsley

sea salt and freshly ground black pepper

Serves 6

Italy is the land of comforting soups, and this one from Campania combines two of the great storecupboard stand-bys—beans and pasta. This is guaranteed to bring tears of homesickness and a smile to the face of any expat Italian when they imagine it. Everyone's *nonna*'s version is THE best. The baking soda helps to soften the beans and dispel any unpleasant after effects—don't add salt and freshly ground black pepper when cooking the beans initially as it will toughen them.

Put the beans in a bowl, cover with cold water, add the baking soda, and leave to soak overnight. Drain just before you're ready to use them.

The next day, put the drained beans in a large saucepan. Add the olive oil, garlic, and stock. Bring to a boil, reduce the heat, and simmer, partially-covered with a lid, for 1–2 hours or until the beans are tender.

Working in batches if necessary, blend the beans with the cooking liquid using a blender or food processor. Return the bean purée to the rinsed-out pan, adding extra water or stock as necessary.

Add the pasta and simmer gently for 15 minutes, until tender. (Add a little extra water or stock if the soup is looking too thick.) Stir in the tomatoes and parsley and season well with salt and pepper. Ladle into warmed serving bowls and add an extra trickle of olive oil. Serve immediately.

summer clam and zucchini soup
acquacotta di mare

1½ lb. fresh baby clams or cockles in their shells, cleaned

3 tablespoons extra virgin olive oil

1 large garlic clove, finely chopped

1½ lb. zucchini, roughly grated

finely grated peel and freshly squeezed juice of 1 lemon

1 tablespoon freshly chopped marjoram, oregano, or nepitella (see recipe introduction)

1 quart vegetable stock (see pages 50–51) or water

to serve:

4 thick slices country bread, toasted

1 large garlic clove, peeled and bruised

extra virgin olive oil

sea salt and freshly ground black pepper

Serves 4

This is a light summery soup of zucchini and clams from coastal Tuscany called *acquacotta* or "cooked water." It is the simplest of soups involving very few ingredients. In the country it would be made more substantial by ladling over toasted bread, to take the edge off your appetite. Many versions are made according to what is available. Farm workers cooked this in a bucket over a fire when out working in the fields. They would add whatever was to hand—perhaps some *nepitella*—a wild herb much like catmint. *Acquacotta di Monte* might have porcini mushrooms and a bit of sausage in it.

Put the clams in a large saucepan and set over a high heat. Cover and cook for a few minutes until they open. Take off the heat, tip into a colander placed over a bowl to catch the juices. Reserve the juice and remove half the clams from their shells, keeping the remaining clams in their shells.

Heat the olive oil in the same saucepan and add the chopped garlic. Cook gently until golden but not brown. Add the zucchini, lemon peel, and marjoram and turn in the oil and garlic until coated. Pour in the stock, season lightly, and bring to simmering point then cover and simmer for about 10 minutes or until the zucchini are cooked. Add the reserved clam juices and the reserved clam meat. Taste and season with salt and pepper, and lemon juice to taste. Gently stir in the reserved clams in their shells and heat through.

To serve, rub the toasted bread with the bruised garlic, place a slice in each bowl, and ladle on the soup. Drizzle each serving with extra olive oil and serve immediately.

chestnut and pancetta soup
minestra di castagne e pancetta

1½ lb. fresh, plump, sweet chestnuts or 14 oz. dried chestnuts, soaked overnight in cold water

1 stick (8 tablespoons) butter

5 oz. pancetta (Italian bacon) or thick-sliced bacon, diced

2 onions, finely chopped

1 carrot, finely chopped

1 celery rib, finely chopped

1 tablespoon freshly chopped rosemary

2 fresh bay leaves

2 garlic cloves, cut in half

sea salt and freshly ground black pepper

Serves 6

I made this robust and chunky soup after gathering fresh sweet chestnuts with Italian friends in the Chianti hills one October afternoon. Preparing the chestnuts is a bit of a chore, but the flavor and texture is wonderful! Use dried chestnuts at a pinch (available from good delicatessens and Italian grocers), or soaked dried chickpeas. Make sure the chestnuts are no more than 1 year old as they can go stale. This soup has a surprisingly sweet taste so you can add a dash of lemon juice, if you like.

Using a small sharp knife, slit the shell of each chestnut across the rounded side. Put the chestnuts in a saucepan and cover with cold water. Bring to a boil and simmer for about 15–20 minutes. Remove from the heat and lift out a few chestnuts at a time. Peel off the outer thick skin, then peel away the inner thinner skin (this has a bitter taste). Alternatively, you can roast the chestnuts in a preheated oven at 400°F for 15 minutes, then peel off both the skins.

Melt the butter in a large saucepan and add the pancetta. Fry over a medium heat until the fat begins to run. Add the onions, carrot, and celery and cook for 5–10 minutes, until beginning to soften and brown. Add the chestnuts to the pan with the rosemary, bay leaves, garlic, and enough water to cover completely.

Bring to a boil, half cover, turn down the heat and simmer for 30–45 minutes, stirring occasionally, until the chestnuts start to disintegrate and thicken the soup. Season to taste with salt and pepper, ladle into warmed serving bowls, and serve.

spinach broth with egg and cheese
minestra di spinaci, uova e parmigiano

1½ lb. fresh leaf spinach

4 tablespoons butter

4 eggs

⅓ cup freshly grated Parmesan cheese

¼ teaspoon freshly grated nutmeg

about 1¾ quarts vegetable or chicken stock (see pages 50–53)

sea salt and freshly ground black pepper

Serves 6

A typical way to thicken and enrich a soup in many parts of Italy is to add beaten eggs. This is one of the best I have tasted because of the freshness of the greens. Although most of us are limited to spinach, there are many more varieties of *ortaggi* (greens) in Italian markets and greengrocers—beet tops, for example, or even zucchini leaves and tendrils. Just outside Modena, this soup was rustled up in minutes for me, as I had arrived too late for anything else. Served with a basket of bread and some homemade salami afterwards, it was just perfect.

Remove all the stalks from the spinach, then wash the leaves thoroughly—do not shake dry. Cook the leaves in a large saucepan with the water still clinging. When the leaves have wilted, drain well, then chop finely.

Heat the butter in a medium saucepan, then add the spinach, tossing well to coat with the butter. Remove from the heat and let cool for 5 minutes.

Put the eggs, Parmesan, nutmeg, salt, and pepper in a bowl and beat well. Mix into the spinach. Put the stock in a large saucepan and bring almost to a boil. When almost boiling, beat in the spinach and egg mixture as quickly as you can to avoid curdling. Reheat gently without boiling for a couple of minutes. Ladle into warmed serving bowls and serve immediately.

pasta, gnocchi, and polenta

1

2

3

4

classic pesto genovese

Don't stint on the fresh basil here—it is instrumental in making this the most wonderful sauce in the world! Adding a little softened butter at the end gives the pesto a creaminess that will help it coat hot pasta. The texture is ideal when the pesto is pounded by hand, so try it once and you'll never make it in a food processor again! Pesto can be frozen successfully—some suggest leaving out the cheese and beating it in when the pesto has thawed, but I have never had any problems including it.

2 garlic cloves
½ cup pine nuts
2 large handfuls basil leaves
⅔ cup extra virgin olive oil, plus extra
for preserving
3 tablespoons unsalted butter, softened
¼ cup freshly grated Parmesan cheese
sea salt and freshly ground black pepper

Makes about 1 cup

(1) Peel the garlic and put it in a mortar with a little salt and the pine nuts. Pound with a pestle until broken up.

(2) Add the basil leaves, a few at a time, pounding and mixing to a paste.

(3) Gradually beat in the olive oil, little by little, until the mixture is creamy and thick. Alternatively, put everything in a food processor or blender and blend until just smooth.

(4) Beat in the butter and season with black pepper, then beat in the Parmesan.

Store in a jar, with a layer of olive oil on top to exclude the air, in the refrigerator until needed, for up to 2 weeks. Level the surface each time you use it, and re-cover the pesto with olive oil.

walnut and caper pesto
pesto alle noci e capperi

Late in the Tuscan summer, my students and I eat lunch in the shade of a huge walnut tree, and we are bombarded with ripe walnuts dropping onto the table. We gathered these small creamy nuts and made this sauce to have with our own spinach tagliatelle and it also goes wonderfully with *topini* (page 87). Fresh walnuts have a rich creamy texture which emulsifies the pesto beautifully. If you can, try using a traditional *mezzaluna* for chopping—once you get the knack you won't turn back!

2 garlic cloves, peeled
⅓ cup walnut halves, fresh if possible
¼ cup salted capers, rinsed
2 oz. flat-leaf parsley leaves
¾ cup extra virgin olive oil, plus extra for preserving
3 tablespoons unsalted butter, softened
4 tablespoons freshly grated pecorino cheese
sea salt and freshly ground black pepper

Serves 4–6

Put the garlic, walnuts, capers, and a little salt in a mortar, then pound with a pestle until broken up. Add the parsley, a few leaves at a time, pounding and mixing to a thick paste. Gradually beat in the olive oil until creamy and thick. Beat in the butter, season with pepper, then beat in the pecorino. Alternatively, blend all of the ingredients in a food processor or blender until smooth.

Store in a jar, with a layer of olive oil on top to exclude the air, in the refrigerator until needed, for up to 2 weeks. Level the surface each time you use it, and re-cover the pesto with olive oil.

pasta, gnocchi, and polenta   73

sauces and sugos

Italian sauces tend to fall into two categories—quick and slow. The quick sauces are the uncooked pestos (see pages 70–73), or sauces made directly in the pan with a wine reduction and perhaps some cream, after cooking a steak or an escalope. These generally are classified as *salse*. *Sugos* on the other hand need long slow cooking to give them their depth of flavor and rich texture. These sauces are the backbone of family cooking in Italy. The majority of *sugos* are started with a pile of finely chopped celery, onion, and carrot (and sometimes garlic) called a *battuto*. These three vegetables are the "holy trinity" of the Italian kitchen. When this vegetable mix is fried in olive oil, it becomes a *soffritto* which forms the aromatic base of the sauce. *Sugos* are normally very fine in texture, the meat being minced very finely before or after cooking. When making a *sugo* it is important not to brown the meat too much or it will turn into hard little bullets, and no matter how long it is cooked, it will never soften again. Half cover and simmer the sauce very slowly indeed, for as long as you have, between 1–3 hours. The longer it simmers the better it will taste. Some tomato *sugos* surround a large piece of meat as it cooks and are served separately mixed with pasta to start the meal, followed by the meat.

rich meat sauce
sugo di carne

This is a classic meat sauce started with a *battuto* (see page 75). Note that the pancetta is added with the minced meat and not fried separately—this makes it blend into the sauce imperceptibly adding its sweet and salty unctuous flavor. When browning the meat and vegetables, cook just enough to turn from raw to cooked so that the meat remains soft and doesn't develop a hard crust. Cook the sauce very slowly indeed, covered with a lid propped up on a wooden spoon placed across the pot.

1–2 oz. dried porcini mushrooms
3 tablespoons butter
2 tablespoons extra virgin olive oil
1 small onion, finely chopped
1 small carrot, finely chopped
1 celery rib, finely chopped
10 oz. lean beef, pork, or veal mince
2 oz. pancetta with plenty of fat, minced, or finely chopped
¼ cup dry red wine
1 lb. passata (Italian sieved tomatoes) or puréed chopped tomatoes
1 tablespoon tomato paste
2 cups meat stock
1 fresh bay leaf
4 oz. plump fresh chicken livers, trimmed and very finely chopped
sea salt and freshly ground black pepper

Serves 4–6

Cover the mushrooms in warm water and leave to soak. Meanwhile, melt the butter in the oil in a flameproof casserole set over medium heat. Add the onion, carrot, and celery and cook for 5–10 minutes until golden, but not brown. Add the meat and pancetta and brown very lightly, breaking up any large lumps. Add the wine, turn up the heat and boil until evaporated. Reduce the heat, then add the passata and the tomato paste, mix well, then add the stock and bay leaf and season with salt and pepper. Bring to a boil, stir well, then half cover, and simmer for about 2 hours, topping up with a little water to prevent it drying out.

After 1½ hours, drain the mushrooms, reserving the liquid, chop finely, and add to the sauce with the chicken livers. Stir well, add a splash of reserved mushroom water, then simmer for a further 30 minutes, or until the butter and oil begins to separate on the surface. It should be rich and thick. Season well and toss with your chosen cooked pasta to serve.

duck sauce from arezzo
sugo aretino

Duck, whether wild or commercially reared, is very popular in this region, in fact all game is highly prized and makes the centerpiece of a winter meal. The commercially available species is the Muscovy duck (*muschiata* or *muta*) and the smaller wild duck are mallard (*germano reale*) and widgeon (*fischione*). Serve this sauce on a pile of steaming polenta or on slices of crispy grilled polenta.

3 tablespoons olive oil
1 whole duck or 2¼ lb. duck joints, including legs and breast
1 onion, finely diced
1 carrot, finely diced
1 celery rib, finely diced
2 garlic cloves, chopped
2½ oz. unsmoked pancetta, finely diced
1¼ cups dry white wine
14-oz. can chopped tomatoes
1¼ cups Chicken Stock (see pages 52–53) or game stock if available
1 oz. dried porcini mushrooms, soaked in warm water for 30 minutes
2 fresh bay leaves
2 tablespoons freshly chopped sage
sea salt and freshly ground black pepper

Serves 4

Heat the olive oil in a sauté pan and fry the duck pieces until golden. Add the onion, carrot, celery, garlic, and pancetta. Stir well and cook gently for about 10 minutes until soft and beginning to brown. Pour in the wine, boil until evaporated, then add the tomatoes and stock, mixing well and scraping away any sediment lodged on the base of the pan. Drain the mushrooms and add to the pan with the herbs, then bring to a boil. Turn down the heat, half cover and simmer gently for at least 2 hours, topping up with a little water as necessary, until the meat is very tender.

Take the pan off the heat. Lift out the duck pieces, remove the skin, and discard, then pull the meat off the bones and either chop it up or pull into fine shreds. Skim the fat off the surface of the sauce and stir in the duck meat. Taste the sauce, season as necessary with salt and pepper, and reheat. Remove the bay leaves and toss with your chosen cooked pasta to serve.

fiery red pepper sauce
salsa piccante di peperoni

This is a rustic sauce for pasta inspired by the delicious spicy pepper dishes made in Elba, the island just off the coast of southern Tuscany. Fresh hot peppers or long chiles (*peperoncini*) are used a lot there, whether red or green. It's a good idea to use rubber gloves when preparing chiles.

6 sweet red bell peppers, cut in half, and seeded
2 large fresh red chiles, cut in half, and seeded
¼ cup extra virgin olive oil
2 garlic cloves, finely chopped
4 ripe tomatoes, chopped
2 tablespoons freshly chopped basil
sea salt and freshly ground black pepper

Serves 4

Cut the peppers into medium dice and finely chop the chiles. Heat the olive oil in a skillet and add the garlic. Cook for 1 minute until golden but not brown. Stir in the peppers and chiles and cook slowly for about 20 minutes until really soft.

Add the tomatoes, season with salt and pepper, then half cover and simmer gently for 20 minutes, until well-reduced, soft and thick. You may have to add a little water to keep the sauce from sticking. Stir in the basil and toss with your chosen cooked pasta to serve.

mushroom and tomato sauce
sugo di funghi e pomodori

If you are lucky enough to have an abundant supply of fresh wild porcini mushrooms in late summer/autumn, then this is the sauce to make. Italians are crazy for porcini (little pigs) and spend hours of their spare time foraging on bosky hillsides—it is seen as their birthright. The porcino's companion herb, *nepitella,* grows wild where the mushrooms are found and is frequently added to your market porcini purchase. A mixture of mint, thyme, and oregano would be a decent substitute. However, for those not living in the land of the mushroom, you can conjure up the same pungent flavor by using a mixture of open-cup mushrooms mixed with a handful of soaked dried porcini and this herb mixture.

10 oz. fresh porcini or large open-cup cultivated mushrooms
⅓ cup extra virgin olive oil
1 oz. dried porcini mushrooms, soaked in warm water for 30 minutes
3 garlic cloves, finely chopped
1 lb. fresh ripe tomatoes or 1 lb. canned chopped tomatoes
1 teaspoon mixed dried mint, oregano, and thyme
sea salt and freshly ground black pepper

Serves 4

Clean the wild mushrooms by brushing them lightly with a pastry brush to remove any grit or dried leaves. Trim the bases of the stems. Wipe the cultivated mushrooms but do not peel or wash. Pull the caps from the stalks and chop them all into small dice.

Heat the olive oil in a large saucepan and add both the fresh and soaked dried mushrooms and the garlic. Toss over a fairly high heat for 2–3 minutes. Add the tomatoes and herbs and season well with salt and pepper. Bring to a boil then half cover and simmer for 20 minutes, or until the oil starts to separate on the surface and the sauce is reduced. Taste and check the seasoning and toss with your chosen cooked pasta to serve.

making basic pasta dough

Nothing beats homemade pasta—not even store-bought "fresh." The texture is silky and the cooked dough itself very light. These quantities are only guidelines—depending on humidity, type of flour used etc, you may have to add more or less flour. I like to use a mixture of 50% Italian "00" flour and 50% *Farina di Semola* (pale yellow, finely ground, hard durum wheat flour for making pasta and some breads—fine Farola baby food is semolina flour). This mixture of soft and hard wheat flours gives the dough a firmer texture. You may also use bread flour. The dough must not be too soft—it should require some serious effort when kneading! However, too much extra flour will make the pasta too tough to handle (or put through the pasta machine) and when cooked, taste floury. Generally allow one egg to ¾ cup flour quantity per portion for a main course. However, it is not really worth the effort making a single quantity—make a large batch and once cut and shaped you can freeze what you do not use. I prefer to make the dough by hand—if you throw everything into a food processor you could end up with a gloopy mess or little dry bullets.

1⅔ cups all-purpose flour (or use Italian "00" flour)
a pinch of sea salt
1 tablespoon olive oil
2 medium eggs

Serves 2–4, depending on size of portion

To make the pasta the traditional way, sift flour onto a clean work surface (some home cooks keep a special wooden pasta board for this) and make a well in the center with your fist.

(1) Break the eggs into the well and add a pinch of salt and freshly ground black pepper and the oil.

(2) Gradually mix the eggs into the flour with the fingers of one hand, and bring it together into a firm dough. If the dough looks too dry, add a few drops of water, if too wet—more flour. You will soon get to know your dough!

(3) Knead the pasta until smooth, lightly massage it with a hint of olive oil, put into a plastic food bag, and allow to rest for at least 30 minutes before attempting to roll out. The pasta will be much more elastic after resting.

(4) Roll out by hand with a long wooden rolling pin or use a pasta machine (see page 80).

Cook's tip: The Italian way is ALWAYS to toss the cooked, hot pasta with the sauce before serving.

1 **2** **3** **4**

Spinach pasta Proceed as with Basic Pasta Dough (left), sift 1⅔ cups all-purpose flour (this flour weight is approximate, you may need a little more to make a firm dough) onto a clean work surface. Blend ¾ cup frozen leaf spinach (cooked and squeezed of as much moisture as possible) with a pinch salt and pepper and 1 medium egg, until very smooth, and continue as for the basic recipe.

Tomato pasta Add 2 tablespoons tomato paste or sun-dried tomato paste to the well in the flour. Use 1 large egg instead of 2 medium ones.

Beet pasta Add 2 tablespoons grated cooked beet to the well in the flour. Again, use 1 large egg instead of 2 medium ones.

Saffron pasta Soak a sachet of powdered saffron in 2 tablespoons hot water for 15 minutes. Use 1 large egg instead of 2 medium ones and beat in the saffron water.

Herb pasta Add at least 3 tablespoons finely chopped fresh green herbs to the well in the flour. Or blanch the herbs, dry, then chop before use.

Black squid ink pasta Add 1 sachet of squid ink to the eggs before adding to the flour. A little extra flour may be needed.

cooking pasta

Cooking times for both fresh and dried pasta vary according to the size and quality of the pasta. The only way to be sure is to taste it (and be guided by the manufacturer's instructions). However, the basic method of cooking remains the same.

Throw the pasta into a large saucepan of boiling, salted water—as a guide, you will need about 4 quarts of water and 3 tablespoons of salt for every 13 oz.–1 lb. 2 oz. fresh or dried pasta. It is this large volume of water that will prevent the pasta from sticking together. Stir once or twice—if you have enough water in the pan and you stir the pasta as it goes in, it shouldn't stick. DO NOT COVER, or the water will boil over. Quickly bring the pasta back to a rolling boil, stir and boil until *al dente* or firm to the bite. It should not have a hard center or be soggy and floppy. Calculate the cooking time from the moment the pasta starts to boil again and have a colander ready.

Drain the pasta, holding back 2–3 tablespoons of the cooking water (a real Italian top tip!), returning the pasta to the pan (the dissolved starch in the water helps the sauce to cling to the pasta). Dress the pasta straight away with the sauce directly in the pan. Serve hot pasta immediately.

using a pasta machine

Feed the rested dough 4–5 times through the widest setting of a pasta machine, folding in three each time, and feeding the open ends through the rollers to push out any air. This will finish the kneading process and make the pasta silky smooth.

Next, pass the pasta through the machine, starting at the widest setting first, then reducing the settings, one by one, until reaching the required thickness. The pasta sheet will become very long—so if you are having trouble, cut in it two and feed each half separately.

Generally the second from last setting is best for tagliatelle, the finest being for ravioli or pasta that is to be filled—but this depends on your machine.

Once the required thickness is reached, hang the pasta over a broom handle or the back of a chair to dry a little—this will make cutting it easier in humid weather, as it will not be so sticky. Alternatively, dust with a little flour and lay out flat on clean kitchen towels. Ravioli should be made straight away as it needs to be soft and slightly sticky to cut, fill, and enclose.

To finish, pass the pasta through the chosen cutters (tagliolini, tagliatelle, etc) then drape the cut pasta over the broom handle again to dry a little and lose any stickiness, until ready to cook. Alternatively, toss the cut pasta lightly in flour (preferably semolina flour) and lay out in loose bundles on a tray lined with a clean kitchen towel. Use as soon as possible before it sticks together.

making pasta shapes by hand

Tagliatelle and its endless width variations (see right): Roll the pasta dough out thinly on a lightly floured surface or roll out using a pasta machine. (1) Roll or fold one end loosely towards the center of the sheet, then do the same with the other so that they almost meet in the middle. Lift one folded side on top of the other—do not press down on the fold. (2) Working quickly and deftly with one motion, cut into thin slices with a sharp knife, down the length of the folded pasta. (3) Immediately unravel the slices (or they will stick together) to reveal the pasta ribbons—you can do this by inserting the back of a large knife and shaking them loose. Hang to dry a little before cooking or (4) dust well with semolina flour and arrange in loose "nests" on a basket or a tray lined with a clean kitchen towel.

Pappardelle: Roll the pasta dough out thinly on a lightly floured surface or roll out using a pasta machine. Using a fluted pastry wheel, cut into wide ribbons. Hang up to dry a little before cooking.

Tortellini: Roll the pasta dough out thinly on a lightly floured surface or roll out using a pasta machine. Using a round cookie cutter, stamp out rounds of pasta. Pipe or spoon your chosen filling into the middle of each round. Brush the edges with beaten egg and carefully fold the round into a crescent shape, excluding all air. Bend the two corners round to meet each other and press well to seal. Repeat with the remaining dough. Leave to dry on a floured kitchen towel for about 30 minutes before cooking.

Ravioli: Cut the dough in half and wrap one half in plastic wrap. Roll the pasta out thinly on a lightly floured surface or roll out using a pasta machine. Cover with a clean kitchen towel or plastic wrap and repeat with the remaining dough. Pipe or spoon small mounds (each about 1 teaspoon) of filling in even rows, spacing them at 1½-inch intervals across one piece of the dough. Using a pastry brush, brush the spaces of dough between the mounds with beaten egg. Using a rolling pin, lift the remaining sheet of pasta over the mounds. Press down firmly between the pockets of filling, pushing out any trapped air. Cut into squares with a serrated ravioli/pastry cutter or sharp knife. Transfer to a floured kitchen towel to rest for about 1 hour before cooking.

Macaroni: In Italy *macaroni* is the generic term for any hollow pasta shape. This simple-to-make version is called *garganelle*. Roll the pasta out thinly to a rectangle on a lightly floured surface or roll out using a pasta machine. Cut squares from the pasta sheets and wrap around a pencil or chopstick on the diagonal to form tubes. Slip off and allow to dry slightly on a tray or floured kitchen towel before cooking.

spaghetti with eggplant and tomato sauce
pasta alla norma

I have eaten many variations of this dish in Sicily. It is very rich, but this is balanced by grated *ricotta salata*—ewe's milk ricotta cheese, salted and aged. It is very dry and concentrated, but sharp and salty. The nearest thing I can find to it outside the area is aged pecorino or even feta cheese. Although a very ancient dish, it has been named *alla Norma* by the people of Catania in homage to the composer Vincenzo Bellini, after one of his operas.

3 medium eggplants (round violet ones if possible)

1 lb. very ripe red tomatoes (add 2 tablespoons of tomato paste if not red enough)

3 tablespoons olive oil

3 garlic cloves, chopped

12 oz. spaghetti or spaghettini

3 tablespoons freshly chopped basil

3–4 tablespoons freshly grated *ricotta salata*, aged pecorino or Parmesan cheese, plus extra to serve

sea salt and freshly ground black pepper

vegetable oil, for frying

Serves 4

Cut the eggplants into small dice and put in a colander. Sprinkle with salt and put the colander on a plate. Set aside to drain for 30 minutes.

Meanwhile, dip the tomatoes in boiling water for 10 seconds, then drop into cold water. Slip off the skins, cut in half, and squeeze out and discard the seeds. Chop the flesh coarsely.

Heat the olive oil in a skillet, add the garlic, cook for 2–3 minutes until golden, then add the tomatoes. Cook for about 15 minutes, until the tomatoes start to disintegrate.

Bring a large saucepan of salted water to a boil, add the spaghetti, and cook according to the package instructions, about 8 minutes.

Meanwhile, rinse the eggplants, drain, and pat dry. Heat 1 inch vegetable oil in a separate skillet, add the cubes of eggplant and shallow fry until deep golden brown. Remove and drain on paper towels. Stir into the tomato sauce.

Drain the pasta, reserving 2 tablespoons of the cooking water in the pan and returning the pasta to the hot pan. Stir in the sauce, basil, and grated cheese, season to taste with salt and pepper, and serve immediately with more cheese on the side.

dried pasta

Commercial dried pasta is made from durum wheat semolina (*farina di semola*) mixed with water. Durum wheat is protein-rich due to the hot dry climate in which it is grown—domestically grown durum wheat comes from Campania and Sicily. It has a heavier, more concentrated inner germ than soft wheat (*grano tenero*), and is richer in proteins, minerals, vitamins, and enzymes. It is pale yellow, but can be darker depending on where it is grown. Soft wheat is milled between smooth cylinders and looses the nutritious wheat germ during the process, but durum wheat is cut and milled by grooved cylinders thus retaining the wheat germ in the final semolina. Pasta made from durum wheat semolina is more resilient when it cooks and has a wonderful fragrance that pasta made with ordinary soft wheat flour just doesn't have. According to Italian law, dried pasta must be made with durum wheat flour only—the addition of soft wheat flour is considered total adulteration. However, that all changed after the 1988 EEC regulations came into force. To their dismay, the production of dried pasta with soft wheat flour or a mixture of semolina and soft wheat flour to make a cheaper product, was authorized.

lasagne
lasagne al forno

about 12 sheets dried or fresh lasagne verdi, made from Spinach Pasta (see page 80) rolled out to the second last setting on the pasta machine

½ cup freshly grated Parmesan cheese

ragù:

4 oz. chicken livers (optional, see recipe introduction)

4 tablespoons butter

3 oz. pancetta or dry-cure smoked bacon in a piece, cubed

1 onion, finely chopped

1 carrot, chopped

1 celery rib, trimmed and finely chopped

8 oz. lean ground beef

2 tablespoons tomato paste

¼ cup dry white wine

¾ cup beef stock or water

freshly grated nutmeg

sea salt and freshly ground black pepper

salsa besciamella:

6 tablespoons butter

⅓ cup all-purpose flour

about 2 cups milk

sea salt

a deep baking dish, about 10 x 8 inches, buttered

Serves 4–6

The classic version of this dish is pasta layered with meat sauce and creamy *salsa besciamella* (béchamel sauce). It is very easy to assemble. Make the ragù the day before, and the *besciamella* on the day. If you use fresh pasta, it doesn't need precooking, and is layered up as it is. Just make sure the meat sauce is quite liquid as this will be absorbed into the pasta as it cooks. Traditional ragù contains chicken livers to add richness, but you can leave them out and replace with an additional quantity of ground beef or pork if you prefer.

To make the ragù, trim the chicken livers (if using), removing any fat or gristle. Cut off any discolored bits, which will be bitter if left on. Coarsely chop the livers. Melt the butter in a saucepan, add the cubed pancetta and cook for 2–3 minutes until browning. Add the onion, carrot, and celery and brown these too. Stir in the ground beef and brown until just changing color, but not hardening—break it up with a wooden spoon. Stir in the chicken livers, if using, and cook for 2–3 minutes. Add the tomato paste, mix well, and pour in the wine and stock. Season well with grated nutmeg, salt, and pepper. Bring to a boil, cover, and simmer very gently for as long as you can—2 hours if possible.

To make the besciamella, melt the butter in a medium saucepan. When foaming, add the flour and cook over gentle heat for about 5 minutes without letting it brown. Have a balloon whisk ready. Slice off the heat and add all the milk at once, whisking very well. When all the flour and butter have been amalgamated and there are no lumps, return to the heat and slowly bring to a boil, whisking all the time. When it comes to a boil, add salt, simmer gently for 2–3 minutes. Cover the surface directly with plastic wrap to prevent a skin forming.

Cook the sheets of dried lasagne in a large saucepan of boiling water in batches according to the package instructions. Lift out with a slotted spoon and drain on a clean kitchen towel. Fresh pasta will not need cooking.

Preheat the oven to 350°F. Spoon one-third of the ragù into the buttered baking dish. Cover with 4 sheets of lasagne and spread with one-third of the besciamella. Repeat twice more, finishing with a layer of besciamella covering the whole top. Sprinkle with Parmesan cheese. Bake in the preheated oven for about 45 minutes, until brown and bubbling. Let stand for 10 minutes to settle and firm up before serving.

1

2

3

little potato gnocchi with sage butter
topini

1⅓ lb. floury potatoes

1½ cups all-purpose flour, plus extra for dusting

1 egg, beaten

3 tablespoons butter, melted

2 tablespoons freshly chopped sage

¾ cup finely grated Parmesan cheese

sea salt and freshly ground black pepper

Serves 4

The Italian word *topini* means "little mice," and this is what they are affectionately known as in Tuscany. Only use white-fleshed floury potatoes for gnocchi. New potatoes will make them gluey and chewy. It takes a little practice to make gnocchi really light, as overworking makes them tough. Some expert gnocchi makers make them without any egg at all—do not try this at home!

Cook the potatoes in a pan of boiling water for 20–30 minutes, until very tender, then drain well.

(1) Halve the potatoes and press through a potato ricer, or peel and press through a strainer onto the table or into a bowl. While they are still warm, add 1 teaspoon salt, and the flour.

(2) Make a well in the center and crack in the egg.

(3) Lightly mix together (turn out onto a floured board if you have mixed this in a bowl).

(4) Knead lightly to yield a smooth, soft, slightly sticky dough.

(5) Roll the dough into long "sausages", ¾ inch in diameter.

(6) Cut into 1 inch pieces and shape into corks or pull each one down over the back of a fork to produce the traditional ridged outside and the hollow inside. Lay them on a lightly floured kitchen towel.

Bring a large pan of salted water to a boil. Cook the gnocchi in batches. Drop them into a boiling water and cook for 2–3 minutes, or until they float to the surface. Remove with a slotted spoon immediately they rise and keep hot while cooking the remainder. Meanwhile, mix the butter and the sage in a small bowl, reheat. Taste and season with salt and pepper. Pour the sage butter over the gnocchi, sprinkle with Parmesan, and serve immediately.

4   5   6

roman gnocchi
with herbs and semolina
gnocchi alla romana con le erbe

Soft and golden, these gnocchi are a staple in the Lazio area around Rome. I have added herbs and mustard to the basic mix and like to serve them with roasted rabbit or lamb. Normally they are served with a simple tomato sauce and are a great favorite with children. Did you know that semolina is hard wheat (durum), ground slightly coarser than flour? It is not a special grain on its own.

1 quart whole milk

1⅔ cups semolina

1¾ cups freshly grated Parmesan cheese

1 stick butter

2 egg yolks

1 tablespoon Dijon mustard

2 tablespoons freshly chopped sage

3 tablespoons freshly chopped
flat-leaf parsley

sea salt and freshly ground black pepper

a baking sheet lined with plastic wrap
a 2-inch cookie cutter
an ovenproof dish, about 10 x 8 inches,
well buttered

Serves 4–6

Pour the milk into a saucepan and whisk in the semolina. Bring slowly to a boil, stirring all the time until it really thickens—about 10 minutes (it should be quite thick, like choux paste). Beat in half the Parmesan, half the butter, the egg yolks, mustard, sage, and parsley. Add salt and pepper to taste.

Spread the mixture onto the lined baking sheet to a depth of ½ inch. Let cool and set (this will take about 2 hours).

Preheat the oven to 400°F.

When the gnocchi have set, cut into triangles or circles with the cookie cutter. Spread the chopped trimmings in the bottom of the ovenproof dish. Dot with some of the remaining butter and sprinkle with a little of the remaining Parmesan. Arrange the gnocchi shapes in a single layer over the trimmings. Dot with the remaining butter and Parmesan.

Bake in the preheated oven for 20–25 minutes, until golden and crusty. Let stand for 5 minutes before serving.

gnocchi explained

In Italy, gnocchi (pronounced *nyaw-kee*) come in many guises. The most popular are probably potato gnocchi which originate from the North. Made from mashed and boiled (or baked) potatoes, flour, and egg, these little dumplings are cooked in boiling salted water before being dressed with melted butter, cheese, or sauce. In February, during Verona's Carnevale revellers celebrate *il Bacanal del Gnocco*—the singular gnocco being a pre-Christian symbol of fertility! In Friuli, the potato dough is wrapped around a juicy dark purple plum, boiled, and served with sugar and melted butter.

Gnocchi *alla romana* on the other hand are made by boiling semolina (*farina di semola*) with milk, then cheese, herbs, and other seasonings are added and the whole mass poured into a tray and left to set. Shapes are stamped or cut out of the set paste, arranged in a baking dish and finished off in the oven with more cheese and butter. Another way to use semolina gnocchi paste is to coat shapes in bread crumbs, deep-fry, and serve with a tomato sauce. Gnocco *fritto* is a deep-fried fritter from Reggio Emilia, not to be confused with a *gnocco emiliano*—a type of *focaccia* (bread)!

baked polenta with fontina and pancetta
polenta pasticciata alla valdostana

This polenta dish is typical fare in some of the little family restaurants you come across off-piste when skiing in the mountains. Sometimes it comes with a wild mushroom or venison sauce. Just the stuff to keep the cold out. Say "*alla Valdostana*," and every Italian will know that there's Fontina cheese in the dish. This is one of the oldest cheeses made in the Valle d'Aosta—it is rich and nutty and melts very easily. It is also the basis of a type of fondue called *fonduta*.

2 cups instant polenta (or real polenta flour)

12 oz. Fontina, raclette, or a mixture of grated mozzarella and cheddar cheese

1 cup freshly grated Parmesan cheese

6 oz. thinly sliced smoked pancetta (Italian bacon)

sea salt

a shallow ovenproof dish, about 10 x 8 inches, well buttered

Serves 6

If using instant polenta, cook according to the package instructions, then turn out into a mound on a wooden board and let cool and set.

To make real polenta, bring 1 quart salted water to a boil, then slowly sprinkle in the polenta flour through your fingers, whisking all the time to stop lumps. Cook, stirring with a wooden spoon, for 45 minutes over a low heat and then turn out into a mound on a wooden board and let cool and set as before.

Preheat the oven to 350°F.

Slice the Fontina thinly or grate it. Cut the polenta into slices about ½-inch thick. Arrange a layer of polenta in the ovenproof dish. Top with half the Fontina and half the Parmesan. Add another layer of polenta, then cover with the remaining Fontina and the remaining Parmesan. Finally, add a layer of pancetta. Bake in the preheated oven for 40 minutes, until brown and bubbling and the pancetta is crisp. Serve immediately.

Cook's note: firm polenta is best cut with a thin piece of string pulled taut between the hands or with a sharp oiled knife.

cooking polenta

The basic method always remains the same when cooking polenta, whether it is quick-cook or normal, firm or soft. Only the proportions of polenta to water change—the grade and quality of the meal and fierceness of the heat will define the finished result.

Use a large sturdy pan with room for movement. The traditional polenta stirrer resembles a thick wooden spoon handle, but a stout wooden spatula or spoon works well. For 4 servings of normal polenta, allow 14 oz. polenta and 2 teaspoons of salt per quart of water. Bring the salted water to a rolling boil. Gradually shower in the polenta in a slow and steady stream through the fingers of one hand, stirring vigorously with the other to beat out any lumps. Once all the polenta has been added, turn down the heat. Stir less vigorously for the remainder of the cooking time or until it thickens and falls away from the sides of the pan. Remove the pan from the heat, season, and either tip out onto a wooden board to form a mound or into an oiled container (spreading it out with wet hands), then leave until completely cold. If the polenta is to be soft like mashed potato, beat in boiling water or milk until the consistency is correct and serve immediately.

soft polenta with sausage ragù
polenta con ragù di salsiccia

1 lb. fresh Italian pork sausages or good all-meat pork sausages

2 tablespoons olive oil

1 onion, finely chopped

2 cups passata (Italian sieved tomatoes)

⅔ cup dry red wine

6 sun-dried tomatoes in oil, drained and sliced

sea salt and freshly ground black pepper

2 teaspoons salt

300 g instant polenta

freshly grated Parmesan cheese, to serve

Serves 4

This is a real winter-warmer from the north of Italy, where polenta is the staple carbohydrate. I have been to a polenta night where the steaming soft cereal was poured straight onto a huge wooden board set in the middle of the table. The sauce was ladled into a large hollow in the center of the polenta and everyone gathered round to help themselves directly from the pile—no plates necessary. This is still done in some mountain trattorias.

To make the ragù, squeeze the sausage meat out of the skins into a bowl and break up the meat. Heat the oil in a medium saucepan and add the onion. Cook for 5 minutes, until soft and golden. Stir in the sausage meat, browning it all over and breaking up the lumps with a wooden spoon. Pour in the passata and the wine. Bring to a boil. Add the sun-dried tomatoes. Simmer for 30 minutes or until well reduced, stirring occasionally. Add salt and pepper to taste.

Meanwhile, bring 5½ cups water to a boil with 2 teaspoons salt. Sprinkle in the polenta, stirring or whisking to prevent lumps forming.

Simmer for 5–10 minutes, stirring constantly, until thickened like soft mashed potato. Quickly spoon the polenta into 4 large, warm soup plates and make a hollow in the center of each. Top with the sausage ragù and serve with grated Parmesan cheese.

risotto

risotti

white risotto
risotto in bianco

This is the method for a basic, unflavored risotto without cheese. The method always remains the same, but the ingredients change slightly. Sometimes, instead of plain onion, a *soffritto*—a finely chopped mixture of onion, carrot, and celery—can delicately flavor the base of a risotto. Cubed pancetta is sometimes added at this stage, but must not be allowed to color or it will become tough. Although the stated amount of stock is correct, I like to top it up to 2 quarts just in case the rice becomes too thick (you could use hot water instead). The really important thing is not to rush making a risotto—treat it with love and respect and you will achieve perfect results.

about 6 cups chicken or vegetable stock (see pages 50–53)
1 stick unsalted butter
1 onion, finely chopped
2 cups risotto rice
⅔ cup dry white wine (optional)
sea salt and freshly ground black pepper

Serves 4–6

Note This recipe gives 4 very generous main course servings or 6 smaller servings. I suggest you allow ½ cup rice per person for a generous serving, but less if adding meat or vegetables.

Put the stock in a saucepan and keep at a gentle simmer. (1) Melt half the butter in a separate large, heavy-based saucepan and add the onion. Cook gently for 10 minutes, until soft, golden, and translucent but not browned.

(2) Add the rice and stir until well coated with the butter and heated through (this is called the *tostatura* and the rice should start to crackle slightly).

(3) Pour in the wine, if using—you should hear a *sospiro* (sigh) as it is added. Boil hard until it has reduced and almost disappeared. This will remove the taste of raw alcohol.

(4) Begin adding the stock, a large ladleful at a time, stirring gently until each ladleful has been almost absorbed into the rice. The risotto should be kept at a bare simmer throughout cooking, so don't let the rice dry out—add more stock as necessary. Continue until the rice is tender and creamy, but the grains still firm. This should take 15–20 minutes, depending on the type of rice used—check the package instructions.

Taste and season well with salt and pepper and (5) beat in the remaining butter (this process of beating is called *mantecare*). Sometimes, according to the recipe, grated Parmesan cheese is beaten in with the butter at this stage.

Cover and let rest for a couple of minutes so the risotto can relax and any cheese will melt, then serve immediately. Venetians believe risotto should be served *all'onda* (like a wave), referring to its liquid texture—so you may like to add a little more hot stock just before you serve to loosen it, but don't let the risotto wait too long or the rice will turn mushy.

3

4

5

rice croquettes with tomato sauce
supplì al telefono con sugo di pomodoro

tomato sauce:

½ cup olive oil

2 garlic cloves, chopped

1 teaspoon dried oregano

1¾ lb. fresh tomatoes, skinned and coarsely chopped, or 28 oz. canned chopped tomatoes

sea salt and freshly ground black pepper

supplì:

⅓ recipe White Risotto (page 96) with 2 tablespoons finely grated Parmesan beaten in

2 eggs, lightly beaten

4 oz. mozzarella cheese, cut into 20 cubes

2 slices cooked ham or mortadella, cut into 20 strips

⅔ cup dried white bread crumbs, for coating

light olive oil or vegetable oil, for deep-frying

sea salt

Makes 20

These rice croquettes are real comfort food. When you bite one, you can pull the melted oozing mozzarella into strings that are said to look like telephone lines strung from pole to pole—hence the name, *supplì al telefono*. You can make it with leftover risotto, but it is so good (kids adore it), it is worth making from scratch as an appetizer or a snack.

To make the tomato sauce, heat the olive oil almost to smoking point in a large shallow pan or wok. Standing back (it will splutter if it's at the right temperature), add the garlic, oregano, tomatoes, and pepper. To acquire its distinctive, concentrated, almost caramelized flavor, the tomatoes must fry at a very lively heat in a shallow pan, so cook over a fierce heat for 5–8 minutes, or until the sauce is thick and glossy. Add salt to taste, pass through a food mill or blend in a food processor, then sieve to remove the seeds. Set aside.

Beat the grated Parmesan and eggs into the risotto. Spread the mixture out on a plate and let cool completely, about 1 hour.

Take a large spoonful of risotto and, with damp hands, mould it into an egg shape. Insert your little finger down through the top of the egg but not quite to the bottom, to make a hole inside. Push in a cube of cheese wrapped with a strip of ham and pinch the top over to seal. Roll the egg shape into a fat cylinder, making sure the filling doesn't burst through. Set on a tray while you make the others. Put the bread crumbs in a shallow bowl. Roll the *supplì* in the bread crumbs until evenly coated. At this stage they can be covered and left in the refrigerator for up to 1 day.

Heat the light olive oil in a large saucepan until a crumb will sizzle immediately. Fry 3–4 *supplì* at a time for 4–5 minutes until deep golden. Drain on paper towels, sprinkle with salt, and serve immediately with warm tomato sauce (or keep warm in a low oven for up to 15 minutes).

butternut squash, sage, and chile risotto
risotto alla zucca, salvia e peperoncino

about 6 cups chicken or vegetable stock (see pages 50–53)

1 stick unsalted butter

1 large onion, finely chopped

1–2 fresh or dried red chiles

1 lb. fresh butternut squash or pumpkin (or rutabaga), peeled and finely chopped (2½ cups)

2⅓ cups risotto rice

3 tablespoons freshly chopped sage

¾ cup freshly grated Parmesan cheese

sea salt and freshly ground black pepper

Serves 6

I live in Scotland and was tempted to make a traditional pumpkin risotto using what we call "turnip" (rutabaga) instead. I was impressed with the result. It was less sweet and cloying than it would be using pumpkin or squash, but had a very distinct flavor. I have served this on Burns' Night on 25th January with haggis, and it is delicious—to my taste anyway—but stick to the traditional recipe and it will be just as good. This tastes wonderful on its own or served with grilled meats, such as pork.

To chop the fresh chiles, if using, (1) halve each chile lengthwise and scrape out the seeds with the back of a knife. (2) Cut the chile into long shreds. (3) Gather the shreds into a bundle and cut across into fine dice. Set aside until needed.

Pour the stock into a saucepan and keep at a gentle simmer. Melt half the butter in a separate large, heavy saucepan and add the onion. Cook gently for 10 minutes, until soft, golden, and translucent but not browned. Stir in the chopped chiles and cook for 1 minute. Add the squash, and cook, stirring constantly for 5 minutes, until it begins to soften slightly. Stir in the rice to coat with the butter and vegetables. Cook for just a few minutes to toast the grains.

Begin adding the stock, a large ladleful at a time, stirring gently until each ladleful has almost been absorbed. The risotto should be kept at a bare simmer throughout cooking, so don't let the rice dry out—add more stock as necessary. Continue until the rice is tender and creamy, but the grains are still firm and the squash is beginning to disintegrate. (This should take about 15–20 minutes depending on the type of rice used—check the package instructions.)

Taste and season well with salt and pepper then stir in the sage, remaining butter, and all the Parmesan. Cover, let rest for a couple of minutes, then serve immediately.

Cook's note: You may like to wear disposable gloves for chopping the chiles—they can irritate the skin, causing a burning sensation on contact.

1   2   3

wild mushroom risotto
risotto ai funghi di bosco

6 cups chicken or vegetable stock
(see pages 50–53)

1 stick unsalted butter

1 large onion, finely chopped

2 garlic cloves, finely chopped

3 cups mixed wild mushrooms, cleaned and
coarsely chopped (or a mixture of wild and
fresh, or 1½ cups cultivated mushrooms, plus
1 oz. dried porcini soaked in warm water
for 20 minutes, drained and chopped)

1 tablespoon each of freshly chopped thyme
and marjoram (or *nepitella*)

⅔ cup dry white wine or vermouth

2⅓ cups risotto rice

¾ cup freshly grated Parmesan cheese,
plus extra to serve

sea salt and freshly ground black pepper

Serves 6

We make this risotto in our cooking classes in Tuscany in October, when fresh
porcini mushrooms are around—and it's a great favorite. Any kind of fresh
wild mushroom will make this taste wonderful—black trompettes de mort,
deep golden girolles, or musky chanterelles. However, it can be made very
successfully using a mixture of cultivated mushrooms and dried reconstituted
Italian porcini or French cèpes. In Italy, a wild herb called *nepitella* is often
used when cooking wild mushrooms. It is a type of wild catmint and
complements the mushrooms very well.

Put the stock in a saucepan and keep at a gentle simmer. Melt the butter in a separate
large, heavy saucepan and add the onion and garlic. Cook gently for 10 minutes, until soft,
golden, and translucent but not browned. Stir in the mushrooms and herbs, then cook over
a medium heat for 3 minutes to heat through. Pour in the wine and boil hard until it has
reduced and almost disappeared. This will remove the taste of raw alcohol. Stir in the rice
and fry with the onion and mushrooms until dry and slightly opaque.

Begin adding the stock, a large ladleful at a time, stirring until each ladleful has been
absorbed by the rice. Continue until the rice is tender and creamy, but the grains still
firm. (This should take 15–20 minutes, depending on the type of rice used—check the
package instructions.)

Taste and season well with salt and pepper. Stir in the Parmesan, cover and let rest for
a couple of minutes. Serve immediately with extra grated Parmesan.

mozzarella and sun-blushed tomato risotto with basil
risotto con mozzarella e pomodori semi-secchi

about 6 cups chicken or vegetable stock (see pages 50–53)

1 stick unsalted butter

1 onion, finely chopped

2 cups risotto rice

⅔ cup dry white wine

8 oz. mozzarella cheese, cut into ½-inch cubes

¼ cup freshly chopped basil, plus extra leaves to serve

10 oz. sun-blushed tomatoes

sea salt and freshly ground black pepper

freshly grated Parmesan cheese, to serve

Serves 4

When you dip your fork into this risotto, you will come across pockets of melting mozzarella. Mix in the tomato topping and you will make more strings. Do try to use mozzarella *di bufala*—it has a fresh, lactic bite well-suited to this recipe.

Put the stock in a saucepan and keep at a gentle simmer. Melt half the butter in a separate large, heavy saucepan and add the onion. Cook gently for 10 minutes, until soft, golden and translucent but not browned. Add the rice and stir until well coated with the butter and heated through. Pour in the wine and boil hard until it has reduced and almost disappeared. This will remove the taste of raw alcohol.

Begin adding the stock, a large ladleful at a time, stirring gently until each ladleful has almost been absorbed by the rice. The risotto should be kept at a bare simmer throughout cooking, so don't let the rice dry out—add more stock as necessary. Continue until the rice is tender and creamy, but the grains still firm. (This should take 15–20 minutes, depending on the type of rice used—check the package instructions.)

Taste and season well with salt and pepper and beat in the remaining butter. You may like to add a little more hot stock at this stage to loosen the risotto. Fold in the cubed mozzarella and chopped basil. Cover and let rest for a couple of minutes so the risotto can relax and the cheese melt. Carefully ladle into warm bowls and put a pile of tomatoes in the centre of each one. Top with basil leaves and serve immediately with a bowl of grated Parmesan.

seafood risotto
risotto ai frutti di mare

13 oz. raw shell-on shrimp

6 cups hot fish stock or Quick Shrimp Stock (see page 138)

1¼ cups dry white wine

6 baby squid, cleaned

6 fresh sea (diver) scallops

1 lb. fresh mussels, in their shells

10 oz. small fresh clams, in their shells

6 tablespoons unsalted butter

1 onion, finely chopped

2⅓ cups risotto rice, preferably *carnaroli*

3 tablespoons freshly chopped flat-leaf parsley, to serve

sea salt and freshly ground black pepper

Serves 6

Make this risotto with whatever seafood you can find, but make it as varied as possible. Cooking the seafood in the stock before making the risotto will intensify its flavor. Italians do not generally serve grated Parmesan with seafood, so don't ask for any in a restaurant—it may be frowned on.

Pull off the shrimp heads and put them in the stock with the wine, bring to a boil, cover, and simmer for 20 minutes. Cut the squid into rings and trim the tentacles. Remove the hard white muscle from the side of each scallop and separate the white flesh from the orange coral. Scrub the mussels well and pull off any beards. Discard broken ones and any that don't close when sharply tapped against a work surface. Rinse the clams well.

Strain the stock into a clean pan and heat to simmering point. Add the shrimp and cook for 2 minutes. Add the squid, scallops, and corals and cook for a further 2 minutes. Remove them all with a slotted spoon and set aside. Put the mussels and clams into the stock and bring to a boil. Cover and cook for 5 minutes or until all the shellfish have opened. Remove with a slotted spoon and set aside.

Melt the butter in a separate large, heavy saucepan and add the onion. Cook gently for 10 minutes, until softened but not browned. Add the rice and stir until well coated with butter and heated through. Begin to add the hot stock, a ladleful at a time, stirring until each ladleful has been absorbed. Continue until all but 2 ladles of stock are left, and the rice is tender but still has some bite to it. This should take 15–20 minutes. Season to taste with salt and pepper. Finally, stir in the remaining stock and all the seafood and cook gently with the lid on for 5 minutes or until hot. Sprinkle with parsley and serve immediately.

saffron risotto
risotto allo zafferano

This is not to be confused with *risotto alla milanese*, which accompanies the famous dish *osso buco*, enriched with delicious beef bone marrow. However, this recipe does the job very nicely, producing a rich, creamy risotto with the delicate taste of saffron. Saffron powder can also be used, but make sure it is real saffron and not just ground stamens of the safflower (see left). Saffron will always be relatively expensive when bought outside its country of origin, and is a great thing to take home with you if you are visiting Italy or Spain, where it can be found at a good price.

saffron

One of the most expensive spices in the world, derived from the stamens of a particular purple crocus, saffron has been used in cooking since Greek and Roman times. It is cultivated in Abruzzo in Italy. Saffron is sold in little folded waxed paper packages sealed in paper sachets or in little glass phials. Due to its expense, it is kept behind the cold meat and cheese counters in some shops—just ask. Generally, the sachets contain powdered saffron (*zafferano in polvere*) and this is most commonly used in Italy. There is much food snobbishness about only using the stamens (*stimmi*) and not the powder. If of good quality, they are as good as each other.

Fresh powdered saffron should look slightly damp when unwrapped and be a deep orangey red—I use the Italian "*Tre Cuochi*" brand. Saffron powder can be mixed straight into the dish, whereas the stamens need to be soaked in a little warm water or stock to release the color and fragrance. Ignore cheap plastic bags filled with pale orangey yellow powder or short filaments—this is *zafferanone* or *zafferano bastardo*—from the petals of the safflower plant (*cartamo*) and used only for color.

about 6 cups chicken or vegetable stock (see pages 50–53)
1 stick unsalted butter
1 onion, finely chopped
2⅓ cups risotto rice
⅔ cup dry white wine
16 saffron threads or ½ teaspoon ground saffron
¾ cup freshly grated Parmesan cheese
sea salt and freshly ground black pepper

Serves 4–6

Put the stock in a saucepan and keep at a gentle simmer. Melt half the butter in a separate large, heavy saucepan and add the onion. Cook gently for 10 minutes, until soft, golden, and translucent but not browned. Add the rice and stir until well coated with the butter and heated through. Pour in the wine and boil hard until it has reduced and almost disappeared. This will remove any raw alcohol taste.

Begin adding the stock, a large ladleful at a time, adding the saffron after the first ladleful. Stir gently until each ladleful has almost been absorbed by the rice. The risotto should be kept at a bare simmer throughout cooking, so don't let the rice dry out—add more stock as necessary. Continue until the rice is tender and creamy, but the grains still firm. (This should take 15–20 minutes, depending on the type of rice used—check the package instructions.)

Taste and season well with salt and pepper and stir in the remaining butter and all the Parmesan. Cover and let rest for a couple of minutes so the risotto can relax, then serve immediately. You may like to add a little more stock just before serving to loosen it, but don't let the risotto wait around too long or the rice will turn mushy.

fennel and black olive risotto
risotto ai finocchi con olive

fennel and black olive relish:

⅓ cup extra virgin olive oil

1 onion, finely chopped

1 garlic clove, crushed

1 fennel bulb, trimmed and chopped

5 sun-dried tomatoes in oil,
drained and coarsely chopped

1¼ cups oven-dried black (Greek-style) olives,
pitted

1 fresh bay leaf

12 basil leaves, torn

2 tablespoons aniseed liqueur, such
as Sambuca

sea salt and freshly ground black pepper

fennel risotto:

about 1 quart vegetable or chicken stock
(see pages 50–53)

1 stick unsalted butter

1 onion, finely chopped

3 fennel bulbs, trimmed and finely chopped
(green tops included)

finely grated peel of 1 lemon

1½ cups risotto rice

⅔ cup dry white wine

freshly grated Parmesan cheese, to serve

Serves 6

A delicate fennel and lemon risotto with the taste of the Mediterranean stirred in just before serving. I like the rich earthiness of shiny, oven-dried black olives, but if you prefer something less pungent, use large, juicy green olives instead.

To make the relish, heat 2 tablespoons of the olive oil in a medium saucepan and gently cook the onion, garlic, and fennel for a few minutes until softening. Add the sun-dried tomatoes, olives, and bay leaf and continue to cook for 2–3 minutes more. Season to taste with salt and pepper, remove the bay leaf, then stir in the basil. Transfer to a food processor and blend to a coarse texture. Stir in the aniseed liqueur and remaining olive oil. Cover and set aside.

To make the risotto, put the stock in a saucepan and keep at a gentle simmer. Melt half the butter in a separate large, heavy saucepan and add the onion. Cook gently for 5 minutes, until soft, golden, and translucent, but not browned. Stir in the fennel and lemon peel and continue to cook for 10 minutes, until softening. Add the rice and stir until well coated with the butter and heated through. Pour in the wine and boil hard until it has reduced and almost disappeared. This will remove the taste of raw alcohol.

Begin adding the stock, a large ladleful at a time, stirring gently until each ladleful has almost been absorbed by the rice. The risotto should be kept at a bare simmer throughout cooking, so don't let the rice dry out—add more stock as necessary. Continue until the rice is tender and creamy, but the grains still firm and the fennel absolutely tender. (This should take 15–20 minutes, depending on the type of rice used—check the package instructions.)

Taste and season well with salt and pepper and beat in the remaining butter. Cover and let rest for a couple of minutes so the risotto can relax, then serve immediately. Just before serving, you may like to add a little more hot stock to loosen the risotto, but don't let it wait around too long or the rice will turn mushy. Top with the fennel and black olive relish, before serving with grated Parmesan.

pizza and bread
pizza e pane

basic pizza dough

This will make the typical Neapolitan-style pizza—soft and chewy with a crisp crust or *cornicione*. Although true Neapolitan pizzas should have no oil in them, I like to add a tablespoon to the dough to keep it moist and add flavor.

1 cake compressed yeast, 1 packet active dry yeast, or 2 teaspoons quick-rising yeast

½ teaspoon sugar

1 cup hand-hot water

4 cups unbleached all-purpose flour or Italian "0" or "00" grade flour, plus extra for dusting

1 teaspoon fine sea salt

1 tablespoon extra virgin olive oil

Makes 2 medium crust pizzas, each 10–12 inches diameter

(1) In a medium bowl, cream the compressed yeast with the sugar and beat in the hand-hot water (between 105°F/115°F).

(2) Leave for 10 minutes until a light froth forms on the surface. For other yeasts, use according to manufacturer's instructions.

Sift the flour with the salt into a large bowl and make a well in the center. (3) Pour in the yeast mixture, (4) then the olive oil. (5) Mix together with a round-bladed knife, then use your hands until the dough comes together.

Tip out onto a lightly floured surface, wash and dry your hands, then (6) knead briskly for 5–10 minutes until smooth, shiny, and elastic (5 minutes for warm hands, 10 minutes for cold hands!) Don't add extra flour at this stage—a wetter dough is better. If you feel the dough is sticky, flour your hands, not the dough. The dough should be quite soft, but if it is really too soft, knead in a little more flour.

To test if the dough is ready, roll it into a fat sausage, take each end in either hand, lift the dough up, and stretch the dough outwards, gently wiggling it up and down—it should stretch out quite easily, if not, it needs more kneading.

Shape the dough into a neat ball. (7) Put into a lightly oiled bowl, cover with plastic wrap or a damp kitchen towel and leave to rise in a warm, draught-free place until doubled in size—about 1½ hours.

Uncover the dough, punch out the air, then tip out onto a lightly floured work surface. Divide in two and shape into smooth balls. Place the balls well apart on nonstick baking parchment, cover loosely with plastic wrap or dust heavily with flour and leave to rise for 60–90 minutes. Use as desired.

(8) Shape into a neat ball, then roll out on a floured surface to the desired thickness.
(9) Feeling the thickness of the dough.

1

2

3

4

5

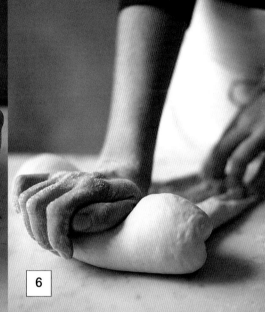

6

7

8

9

the pizza maker's sauce
salsa alla pizzaiola

This is one of the key ingredients of a pizza, and gives it its distinct flavor. It is a speciality of Naples, and much better than anything out of a jar or can. To acquire its distinctive concentrated sweet flavor, the tomatoes must be fried over a very lively heat. Pizzerias have huge food mills to pulp either the tomatoes or sauce, and smaller domestic ones (*passapomodoro*) are available in Italian markets—but a mouli will do at home.

1

2

3

4

5

6

2 lb. fresh tomatoes or
two 14-oz. cans chopped tomatoes
½ cup olive oil
2 garlic cloves, chopped
1 teaspoon dried oregano
sea salt and freshly ground
black pepper

Makes about 1¾ cups

(1) Halve and core the fresh
tomatoes or drain the canned
tomatoes and reserve the juice.

(2) The prepared ingredients.

Heat the oil almost to smoking point
(a wok is good for this) in a large
pan. Standing back (it will splutter),
shoot in the fresh chopped tomatoes
or the drained canned ones. The
juices will caramelize when they hit
the intense heat. Wait for a minute,
then add the remaining ingredients
(remember to add the reserved
tomato juice from the canned
tomatoes), minus the salt. Cook over
a fierce heat for 5–8 minutes, or until
the sauce is thick and glossy, and
the oil is emulsified (3). Season to
taste with salt and pepper.

(4) Pass through a food-mill (mouli)
set over a bowl to remove seeds and
skins. At this stage, you can reduce
it further—the seeds and skins can
make the sauce bitter.

(5) To use, ladle the sauce into the
center of the pizza base and (6)
spread out in a circular motion with
the back of the ladle.

pizza and bread **117**

pizza margherita

½ recipe Basic Pizza Dough (page 114), making just 1 ball of dough

2–3 oz. buffalo mozzarella or cow's milk mozzarella (*fior di latte*)

3–4 tablespoons *Salsa alla Pizzaiola* (see page 116)

6 oz. very ripe cherry tomatoes, halved

a large handful of basil leaves

extra virgin olive oil, to drizzle

sea salt and freshly ground black pepper

a *testo (terra cotta bakestone)* or a large, heavy baking sheet

a pizza peel or rimless baking sheet

Makes 1 medium crust pizza, 10–14 inches diameter

A Neapolitan baker called Raffaele Esposito is said to have been responsible for the birth of modern-day pizza. In 1889, in Naples, he baked three different pizzas for the visit of King Umberto I and Queen Margherita of Savoy. The Queen's favorite was very patriotic, symbolizing the flag of newly unified Italy in its colors of green (basil leaves), white (mozzarella) and red (tomatoes). It was then named Pizza Margherita in her honour and this is it. To be truly authentic, all the ingredients should be local—the basil should really be hand-picked from a Neapolitan balcony!

Put the testo or large, heavy baking sheet on the lower shelf of the oven. Preheat the oven to 425°F for at least 30 minutes.

Lightly squeeze any excess moisture out of the mozzarella, then roughly slice it.

Uncover the pizza dough, punch out the air, and roll or pull it into a 10-inch diameter circle directly onto nonstick baking parchment. Slide this onto the pizza peel or rimless baking sheet. Spread the pizzaiola sauce over the pizza base, leaving a ½-inch rim around the edge. Scatter with the tomatoes and season with salt and pepper.

Working quickly, open the oven door and slide both paper and pizza onto the hot testo or baking sheet. If you are brave, try to shoot the pizza into the oven so that it leaves the paper behind—this takes practice! Bake for 5 minutes, remove from the oven and scatter the mozzarella over the tomatoes. Return the pizza to the oven, this time without the paper. Bake for a further 15 minutes or until the crust is golden and the cheese melted but still white. Remove from the oven, scatter with the basil leaves, and drizzle with olive oil. Serve immediately.

caramelized red onion pizza with capers and olives
pizza con cipolle rosse, capperi e olive

1 recipe Basic Pizza Dough (page 114), dividing the dough into 6–8 balls

2¼ lb. red onions, thinly sliced

freshly squeezed juice of 1 lemon

¼ cup olive oil, plus extra to drizzle

2 teaspoons dried oregano

1 ball of mozzarella, drained and thinly sliced

2 tablespoons freshly grated Parmesan cheese

12 anchovy fillets in oil, drained (optional)

15 black olives, pitted

2 tablespoons capers in salt, washed and drained

sea salt and freshly ground black pepper

2 testi (terra cotta bakestones) or large, heavy baking sheets

2 rimless baking sheets

Makes 4–6 pizzas, depending on size

With no hint of tomato sauce, this is a succulent pizza where the onions are cooked until soft and caramelized, before being spread on the pizza on top of the mozzarella. Olives, capers, and anchovies add savoriness to the sweet onions. You can leave out the anchovies and add tuna or sardines instead.

Put the testi or large, heavy baking sheets on the lower shelf of the oven. Preheat the oven to 425°F for at least 30 minutes.

Toss the onions in the lemon juice to coat them thoroughly. Heat the oil in a large, shallow saucepan and add the onions. Cook over a gentle heat for about 10 minutes, stirring occasionally, until they are beginning to color. Stir in the dried oregano.

Uncover the dough balls, punch out the air, and roll or pull each one into thin circles directly onto separate sheets of nonstick baking parchment. Slide onto 2 rimless baking sheets.

Cover the pizza bases with the mozzarella, leaving a ½-inch rim around the edge. Top with the onions and sprinkle with the Parmesan. Scatter the anchovy fillets (if using), olives, and capers over the top. Drizzle with olive oil, then season with salt and pepper, but don't use too much salt as the capers will be salty.

Working quickly, open the oven door, and slide both paper and pizzas onto the hot testi or baking sheets. Bake for 15–20 minutes or until the crusts are golden. Remove from the oven and drizzle with extra olive oil. Serve immediately.

calzone alla parmigiana

1 recipe Basic Pizza Dough (page 114),
up to the first rising

2 eggplants, diced

12 whole garlic cloves, peeled

¼ cup extra virgin olive oil,
plus extra to glaze

6½ oz. buffalo mozzarella or cow's milk
mozzarella (*fior di latte*)

5 ripe tomatoes, diced

3 tablespoons freshly chopped basil

¼ cup freshly grated Parmesan cheese

sea salt and freshly ground
black pepper

2 large, heavy baking sheets

2 rimless baking sheets

a roasting pan

Makes 4 calzone

This is a good calzone to make for more than two people. The filling ingredients can be chopped as finely or roughly as you like, but the eggplant must be cooked before it goes into the dough. I sometimes add a couple of tablespoons of *Salsa alla Pizzaiola* (see page 116) to the mixture to make it extra tomatoey.

Put the large, heavy baking sheets into the oven. Preheat the oven to 400°F for at least 30 minutes.

Uncover the dough, punch out the air, and divide into 4 balls. Dredge with flour and leave to rise on floured baking parchment for about 20 minutes, until soft and puffy.

Toss the diced eggplant and garlic cloves with the olive oil in a roasting pan and roast for 20 minutes. Lightly squeeze any excess moisture out of the mozzarella, then cut it into cubes. Remove the roasting pan from the oven and cool for 10 minutes before stirring in the tomatoes, mozzarella, and basil. Season to taste with salt and pepper.

Roll or pull the risen balls of dough into 8-inch circles directly onto 2 sheets of nonstick baking parchment. Slide these onto the 2 rimless baking sheets. Spread a quarter of the vegetable mixture on one half of each calzone, leaving just over ½ inch around the edge for sealing. Season well with salt and pepper. Fold the uncovered half of the dough over the filling. Pinch and twist the edges firmly together so that the filling doesn't escape during cooking. Brush with olive oil and sprinkle with Parmesan.

Working quickly, open the oven door and slide both paper and calzone onto the hot baking sheets. Bake for 30 minutes, swapping the baking sheets around halfway through cooking time. When the crusts are puffed up and golden, remove the calzone from the oven and leave to stand for 2–3 minutes before serving.

focaccia with rosemary
focaccia al rosmarino

5 cups Italian "00" grade flour or all-purpose flour, plus extra for kneading

½ teaspoon fine sea salt

1½ cakes compressed fresh yeast (for dried yeast, follow the package instructions)

⅔ cups extra virgin olive oil

2 cups hand-hot water

coarse sea or crystal salt flakes

sprigs of rosemary

2 shallow cake pans, pie or pizza plates, about 10 inch diameter, lightly oiled

a water spray

makes 2 thick focacce, each 10 inches diameter

Focaccia literally means "a bread that was baked on the hearth," but it is easy to bake in conventional ovens. It is found in many different forms, and can be thin and crisp, thick and soft, round or square. I make this one in a pan, but it can be shaped on a baking sheet to any shape you want. A terra cotta bakestone (*testo*) or unglazed terra cotta floor tile heated in the oven will give pizzas and focacce extra lift and a crisp base. Although a rustic focaccia can be made with any basic pizza dough, the secret of a truly light focaccia lies in three risings, and dimpling the dough with your fingers so it traps olive oil while it bakes.

Sift the flour and fine salt into a large bowl and make a hollow in the center. Crumble in the yeast. Pour in 3 tablespoons of the olive oil, then rub in the yeast until the mixture resembles fine bread crumbs. Pour in the hand-hot water and mix with your hands until the dough comes together.

Transfer the dough to a floured surface, wash and dry your hands, then knead the dough for 10 minutes until smooth and elastic. The dough should be quite soft, but if too soft to handle, knead in more flour, 1 tablespoon at a time. Put the dough in a clean, oiled bowl, cover with a damp kitchen towel or plastic wrap and let rise in a warm, draught-free place until doubled in size, about 30 minutes–1½ hours.

Punch down the dough and cut in half. Put on a floured surface and shape each half into a round ball. Roll out into 2 circles, each 10 inches diameter, and put in the oiled tins. Cover with a damp kitchen towel or plastic wrap and let rise for 30 minutes.

Remove the kitchen towel, and (1) using your fingertips, make deep dimples all over the surface of the dough. (2) Pour over all but 2 tablespoons of the oil, re-cover, and leave to rise to the top of the tins—about 30 minutes.

Uncover and spray with water, (3) sprinkle with the rosemary and plenty coarse salt, and bake in the preheated oven for 20–25 minutes until risen and golden brown. Drizzle with the remaining olive oil. Transfer to a wire rack to cool. Eat on the same day or wrap and freeze when cool. Defrost then wrap in foil and reheat in a hot oven for 5 minutes.

1 2 3

biga

Biga is a type of starter used in Italian baking both in the home and in many bakeries. It adds complexity to the bread's flavor and is used in breads which need a light, open texture like ciabatta. Biga is generally made fresh every day, unlike a sourdough starter, and is allowed to ferment for up to 24 hours to develop fully. You will need ⅔ cup warm water (warm means blood temperature—you should be able to hold your finger in the water without any pain!), 1 level tablespoon dry active yeast and 1 scant cup all-purpose unbleached flour, warmed (see Cook's Note, right)

To make the *biga*, pour the warm water into a medium bowl and beat in the yeast beating until dissolved, then gradually beat in all the flour to form a smooth loose batter. Pour into a plastic container and snap on the lid. Leave in a warm place for a minimum of 9 hours and up to 24 hours, after which time it should be alive and slightly frothy/bubbly and smell fantastically yeasty. If the weather is very warm, it may rise then collapse on itself again—don't worry, it will still work. Freeze in ¾ cup portions or keep in the refrigerator in a plastic container for up to 2 weeks.

tuscan saltless bread
pane toscano

Tuscans like heavily seasoned food, but not their bread. It is said that as salt used to be taxed, it was not added to a daily necessity like bread, but kept for preserving meat, vegetables, and fish. I find that it complements Tuscan food very well and is the perfect vehicle for dipping into olive oil as it doesn't compete for taste. This recipe uses a *biga* as a starter, to give the bread a more genuine, slightly sourdough taste. It is easy to make and once you've tried it, you'll never make bread any other way! Using a *biga* gives the pleasant slightly sour taste so characteristic of country breads.

1 recipe Biga (see left)
about ¾ cup warm water
3 cups all-purpose unbleached flour, warmed (see Cook's Note below), plus extra for kneading and shaping

Makes one 1¼ lb. loaf

Transfer the biga to a large bowl and whisk in the warm water. Now mix in the flour gradually until you have a pliable, firm dough (err on the soft side rather than have it too firm). Gather it together in the bowl, making sure all the flour is kneaded in.

Lift out onto a clean floured work surface and knead for 10 minutes. The dough will be a bit stickier than normal, so keep flouring your hands and not the table or dough—you don't want to change the proportions. When the dough begins to become very elastic, it is ready to shape. With one hand, pull the outside edge towards the middle, turning the dough as you go round to form a ball. Flip over onto some flour then pull gently to form a rough rectangle. Flip this over again onto a floured baking sheet so that the rough side is uppermost. Slash along the middle with a very sharp knife. Cover with a large upturned bowl and leave to rise until almost doubled—about 1½ hours.

Place a roasting pan of hot water on the base of the oven and preheat the oven to 400°F. Bake the loaf for 35–40 minutes until it sounds hollow when tapped on the underside. Cool on a wire rack. This will freeze for up to 3 months.

Cook's note: Warming the flour speeds up the reaction of the yeast. You can do this in a microwave oven. Put the flour in a non-metallic bowl and cook on HIGH for 20 seconds. Remove from the oven and fluff up the flour with your fingers—it should feel warm, if not return it to the oven for another 10 seconds or so. Use before it cools, but be warned, if it is too hot it may kill the yeast.

fish and seafood
pesci e frutti di mare

fish baked in a salt crust
pesce in crosta di sale

This excellent and ancient method of cooking fish conserves the juices without in any way oversalting the flesh. The salt bakes hard to form a protective crust so that the fish cooks in its own juices—the skin protects it from the salt. It's a nice idea to stuff the cavity with fresh herbs and lemon slices before burying the fish in salt.

at least 2 lb. fine sea salt

1 egg white

2–4 lb. whole large firm-fleshed fish, cleaned
but not scaled

a tomato salad, to serve (optional)

*a long ovenproof dish (choose one that will
comfortably hold the whole fish)*

Serves 4–6

Preheat the oven to 375°F.

Pour enough salt into the ovenproof dish to make a layer 1 inch thick. Mix the egg white with 3 tablespoons water and sprinkle half the liquid over the salt. Set the fish on the salt bed and pour enough salt around and over it to cover it completely. Sprinkle with the remaining egg white and water mixture.

Bake the fish in the preheated oven for about 45 minutes–1 hour. Remove from the oven and put the dish, with the fish still encased in its snowy armor, in the middle of the table.

Crack open the salt crust with a rolling pin. Remove the shards of salt crust and peel back the skin and scales to reveal perfectly cooked, succulent flesh without a trace of saltiness.

Serve with a simple tomato salad, if liked.

Sicilian sea salt

Sicilian sea salt is my choice of salt. I love the fact that is still made in exactly the same way it has been made since the most ancient of times—in the same stone salt pans. I find the flavor bold, without being too strong or salty if that makes sense! It is produced from the shallow lagoon waters of the Mediterranean on the western coast of Sicily near Trapani. It is a natural untreated salt, still made by traditional methods. The ancient salt pans (made of stone cut and laid by ancient Greek and Roman occupiers) are filled with sea water in the spring and left to evaporate under the intense heat of the Sicilian sun and strong African winds. Windmills drive the huge wooden Archimedes screws that move the ever-concentrating salt water from salt pan to salt pan. It is naturally rich in minerals such as iodine, fluorine, magnesium, and potassium. The salt is harvested by hand once the water has evaporated revealing sparkling salt crystals. The salt is raked into small heaps inside the salt pans and then formed into larger piles along the edges where they are protected from the rain with traditional terra cotta tiles. It is then simply crushed and ground without further refining. Do look out for it in specialty food shops.

1

2

3

spaghetti with mussels, tomatoes and parsley
spaghetti con le cozze

2 lb. live mussels or small clams,
in their shells

½ cup olive oil

1¼ cups dry white wine

16 oz. spaghetti or spaghettini

2 garlic cloves, peeled and crushed

14 oz. can chopped tomatoes

2 tablespoons freshly chopped
flat-leaf parsley

sea salt and freshly ground black pepper

Serves 4

Long pasta is the choice for seafood dishes around coastal Italy—spaghetti and spaghettini in the south. This one is another simple dish made with local ingredients—nothing sophisticated, but it tastes so good. When buying mussels, make sure that when you tap each one sharply against the work surface, it closes—if not, it is dead and should be thrown away. It's a good idea to soak the mussels in cold water overnight to purify them before cleaning them. This dish is equally good made with small clams.

Put the mussels in a bowl of cold water and rinse several times to remove any grit or sand. (1) Pull off the beards (2) then use the back of a knife to remove any barnacles and scrub well under cold running water. (3) Discard any mussels that are not firmly closed. Drain.

Heat the oil and wine in a saucepan and add the mussels. Stir over a high heat until the mussels open. Remove and discard any that don't open.

Lift out the cooked mussels with a slotted spoon and put them in a bowl. Reserve the cooking liquid. Cook the spaghetti with plenty of boiling water according to the package instructions, usually about 8 minutes.

Meanwhile, add the garlic to the mussel cooking liquid in the pan and boil fast to reduce and concentrate the flavor. Stir in the tomatoes, return to a boil, and boil fast for a further 3–4 minutes, until reduced. Stir in the mussels and half the parsley and heat through. Taste and season well with salt and pepper.

Drain the pasta, reserving 2 tablespoons of the cooking water in the pan. Return the pasta to the hot pan and stir in the sauce. Sprinkle with the remaining parsley and serve.

squid sautéed with potatoes and chile
seppie con patate e peperoncino

2 lb. fresh whole squid

⅔ cup extra virgin olive oil

4 garlic cloves, chopped

⅔ cup dry white wine

½–1 teaspoon dried hot red pepper flakes

1¾ lb. yellow-fleshed potatoes, peeled and cut into chunks, or small new potatoes, halved

3 tablespoons freshly chopped parsley

sea salt and freshly ground black pepper

lemon wedges, to serve

Serves 4

There's something about the sweetness of squid and the fire of hot red pepper that marries very well. Small amounts of hot pepper are said to aid the digestion. This dish can be made with ready-cleaned squid, in which case you will need about 5 oz. per person. This is one of the best ways of cooking squid as the long cooking ensures that it is tender.

To clean the squid, pull the head from the body. Remove the "plastic quill" from the inside of the squid tube. Rinse the tubes and slice into rings. Trim the tentacles from the head by holding the head just below the eyes and cutting the tentacles away. Pop out the "beak" from the tentacles. Rinse, discarding the head and entrails.

Heat the oil in a flameproof casserole and add the garlic, cook for about 1 minute, then add the squid and stir-fry for about 1 minute. Pour in the wine and add the pepper flakes.

Bring to a boil, then cover and simmer very gently for 30 minutes—you may have to top up the liquid at least once to prevent it sticking. Stir in the potatoes with ⅓ cup water, season with salt and pepper, cover, and cook very gently for another 25 minutes. Stir well, then sprinkle with parsley and serve immediately with lemon wedges.

shrimp in tomato sauce with chickpea pasta
gamberi con pasta di farina di ceci

Use medium-sized, fresh raw unpeeled shrimp (*gamberi*), but remove the heads before cooking, although Italians prefer them in the sauce so that they can pull off the heads and suck out the juices! (The heads can be used to make a wonderful stock (*rapido di gamberi*) to add to the sauce, see left). This dish can also be made with mixed seafood such as mussels, clams, and squid—whatever is around. Chickpea pasta is made in Southern Italy, sometimes it is cut into pasta ribbons called *laganelle* (slightly wider than fettuccine), and is most often served with fish, shrimp, or squid.

chickpea pasta:
1½ cups chickpea flour or gram flour
1½ cups all-purpose flour
5 eggs
extra virgin olive oil, for tossing

shrimp sauce:
3 garlic cloves, finely chopped
3 tablespoons extra virgin olive oil
1 fresh hot red chile, seeded and finely chopped
or a generous pinch of chili powder
1 lb. ripe tomatoes, peeled and chopped
(use halved cherry tomatoes in season)
1 cup dry white wine
½ cup Quick Shrimp Stock (see left)
7 oz. canned chickpeas, rinsed and drained
1–2 teaspoons sugar, to taste
1 lb. raw tiger shrimp, shelled and deveined
4 tablespoons freshly chopped flat-leaf parsley,
plus extra to garnish
sea salt and freshly ground black pepper

Serves 4–6

Make up the pasta dough as for Basic Egg Pasta on page 78 and cut into tagliatelle. Note that chickpea flour pasta is very delicate, and is better rolled out slightly thicker than normal.

To make the shrimp sauce, fry the garlic in the oil until it just begins to color. Add the chile and tomatoes, and cook for 5 minutes. Add the wine and stock. Season with salt and pepper, add the chickpeas and sugar and simmer for 10 minutes to reduce by half. Add the shrimp and simmer for 3 minutes, then stir in the parsley.

Meanwhile, cook the pasta in plenty of boiling salted water for 1 minute. When cooking, don't stir too much or it will break up—handle it gently. It is ready when the water comes back to a rolling boil. Drain the pasta and toss lightly with a little olive oil. Serve with the shrimp sauce and sprinkle with chopped parsley.

quick shrimp stock

This recipe uses shrimp heads that you would normally discard. The stock is quite sweet, unlike one made with fish.

1 onion or ½ leek, chopped
1 celery rib with leaves, chopped
a few parsley stalks, lightly crushed
2 fresh bay leaves
2 lemon slices
4 black peppercorns
¼ cup dry white wine
a generous pinch of sea salt
about 2 lb. raw shrimp heads

Makes 2 quarts

Put all the ingredients except the shrimp heads in a large stockpot. Add enough water to cover and bring to a boil. Turn down as soon as it is boiling, and simmer for 15 minutes. Stir the stock and skim, then add the shrimp heads. Slowly return to a boil, then turn down the heat and cook at the barest simmer for 15 minutes, skimming often. Remove from the heat and strain into a bowl through a colander lined with cheesecloth. Discard the colander contents. Cool the stock and refrigerate for several hours. Now you can either reboil the stock to concentrate it, or cover and refrigerate or freeze until needed. The stock will keep in the refrigerator for 1–2 days or frozen for up to 3 months.

a big fish stew
brodetto di pesce

1 lb. small fresh squid, cleaned

8 raw shrimp tails (optional)

2 lb. fresh mussels and clams*, in their shells

3½ lb. mixed whole but cleaned fish
(see note on fish choice)

flavored broth:

⅔ cup extra virgin olive oil

4 medium leeks, sliced and well washed

4 garlic cloves, finely chopped

1¼ cups dry white wine

a large pinch of saffron threads

½ lb. ripe red plum tomatoes,
coarsely chopped

2 tablespoons sun-dried tomato paste or
purée or 6 sun-dried tomatoes in oil, drained
and coarsely chopped

1 teaspoon fennel seeds

1 tablespoon dried oregano

sea salt and freshly ground black pepper

to serve:

lemon wedges

handfuls of freshly chopped flat-leaf parsley

crusty bread

Serves 6–8

Scrub and debeard the mussels (see page 134). Discard any that don't close—they are dead—and also any with damaged shells. Keep them in a bowl of cold water until ready to cook.

On Fridays and market days, fish is the best thing to buy. Cooked in a big quantity, this stew is the perfect family feast and so typical of many coastal *trattorie*. Try to include a good selection of fish—in Italy, there are boxes of fish on market stalls labelled *per zuppa*, which means small or bony fish with lots of flavor, only for soups or stews. A well-flavored base broth is essential, and should include saffron and fennel seeds. The fish is then poached in this stock. The fish is served separately and the broth is ladled on top.

To make the broth, heat the olive oil in a large, deep soup kettle and add the leeks and garlic. Cook gently for about 5 minutes, until softened. Pour in the white wine and boil rapidly until reduced by half. Add the saffron, tomatoes, tomato paste, fennel seeds, and oregano. Pour in 2¾ cups water and bring to a boil. Turn down the heat, cover, and simmer for 20 minutes, until the tomatoes and oil separate.

Start cooking the fish. Add the squid to the broth and poach for 3–4 minutes. Remove with a slotted spoon, put on a plate, cover, and keep them warm. Add the shrimp tails, if using, and simmer just until opaque. Remove with a slotted spoon and keep warm with the squid. Add the mussels and clams to the broth, cover, and boil for a few minutes until they open. Remove with a slotted spoon and keep them warm. Discard any that haven't opened.

Poach all the remaining fish in the broth until just cooked, remove from the broth, arrange on a serving dish, and set the mussels, squid, and shrimp on top. Taste the broth, which will have all the flavors of the cooked fish in it, and add salt and pepper if necessary. Moisten the fish with some broth and serve the rest separately with the lemon wedges, parsley, and crusty bread.

Fish choice: Choose at least 4 varieties of fish—the greater the variety, the more intense the flavor. Do not choose oily fish like salmon or bluefish. Choose from: clams (*vongole*), mussels, lobster (*aragosta*), raw shrimp, squid, cod, grouper, halibut, monkfish, sea bass, shark, swordfish, tilefish, or whiting.

sea bass baked in parchment
branzino al cartoccio

2 fresh sea bass, about 12 oz. each, cleaned and scaled

4 fresh bay leaves

a few of sprigs of fresh thyme

6 thin slices of lemon

a little freshly squeezed lemon juice or dry white wine

extra virgin olive oil, for brushing and drizzling

sea salt and freshly ground black pepper

Serves 2

Sea bass has a wonderful, clean, fresh taste and this is possibly the best way to cook whole fish (with the possible exception of grilling over embers). The parchment lets the fish steam in its own juices, absorbing the aroma of the fresh herbs and lemon. This cooking time should be perfect—the fish is better to be slightly under-done at the bone than over-done. The packages should be opened at the table to appreciate the full aroma.

Preheat the oven to 375°F.

Cut two large ovals of nonstick baking parchment big enough to wrap each fish generously in a half moon. Brush the parchment with a little oil.

Lay each fish on one half of each sheet of parchment. Season the cavities with salt and pepper. Place two bay leaves in the cavity of each fish and (1) tuck in the thyme sprigs and lemon slices. (2) Drizzle with olive oil and (3) squeeze over the lemon juice.

(4) Fold the remaining half of the parchment loosely over the fish, then (5) twist or fold the edges tightly together to seal and (6) finish with a final twist. Repeat with the other fish. Put both packages on a baking sheet. Bake in the preheated oven for 20 minutes. Serve immediately, opening the packages at the table.

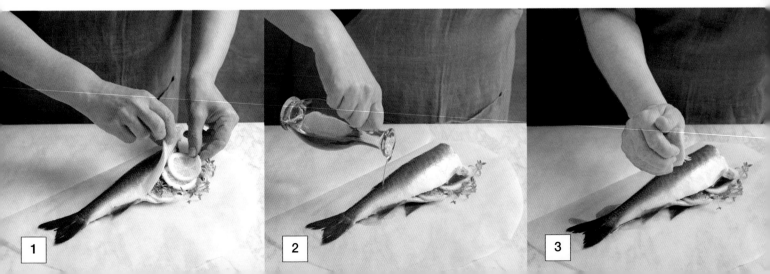

1   2   3

4

5

6

grilled sardines
with salmoriglio sauce
sarde alla griglia con salmoriglio

12 fresh fat sardines

olive oil

lemon wedges, to serve

salmoriglio sauce:

2 tablespoons red wine vinegar

1–2 teaspoons sugar

finely grated peel and freshly squeezed juice of ½ lemon

¼ cup extra virgin olive oil

1 garlic clove, finely chopped

1 tablespoon dried oregano, crumbled

1 tablespoon salted capers, rinsed and chopped

a barbecue grill rack

Serves 4

The smell of silvery blue sardines on a grill is unmistakable—it is one of the most appetizing scents in outdoor cooking. Sardines grill very well because they are an oily fish and are self-basting. Great shoals of them are to be found in Mediterranean waters in May and June, which is the best time to eat them. They are eaten grilled or fried, boned or stuffed, always *con gusto*!

To make the salmoriglio sauce, put the vinegar and sugar in a bowl and stir to dissolve. Add the lemon peel and juice. Whisk in the olive oil, then add the garlic, oregano, and capers. Set aside to infuse.

Using the back of a knife, scale the sardines, starting from the tail and working toward the head. Slit open the belly and remove the insides, then rinse the fish and pat dry. Clip off any fins you don't want to see. Paint the fish with olive oil and arrange on a grill rack (there are racks especially made in a wheel shape for sardines).

Cook under a preheated hot broiler or over glowing barbecue coals for about 3 minutes on each side, until sizzling hot and charring. Serve with the salmoriglio sauce spooned over the top, with lots of lemon wedges alongside for squeezing.

grilled tuna steaks
with peperonata
tonno alla griglia con peperonata

4 fresh tuna loin steaks, cut ½ inch thick

olive oil, for cooking

marinade:

4 garlic cloves, peeled

3 tablespoons Dijon mustard

2 tablespoons grappa or brandy

sea salt and freshly ground black pepper

peperonata:

⅓ cup olive oil

2 lb. fresh ripe tomatoes, peeled, seeded, and chopped, or 28 oz. canned chopped tomatoes

½ teaspoon hot red pepper flakes

2 onions, thinly sliced

3 garlic cloves, chopped

3 large red bell peppers, halved, seeded, and cut into thin strips

sea salt and freshly ground black pepper

Serves 4

Tuna is a very rich meat and is always cut thinly in Italy—never as thick as the seared steaks we are used to. Marinating the slices in mustard and grappa gives them a piquant crust—so good with the sweet bell peppers. Over-cooking tuna can make it very dry, so watch it like a hawk.

To make the marinade, crush the garlic, put it in a bowl, and beat in the mustard and grappa. Season with salt and pepper and use to spread over the cut sides of the tuna. Arrange in a non-reactive dish, cover, and let marinate in a cool place for about 1 hour.

To make the peperonata, heat 3 tablespoons of the oil in a saucepan, then add the tomatoes and pepper flakes. Cook over a medium heat for about 10 minutes, or until the tomatoes disintegrate.

Heat the remaining oil in a skillet, add the onions, garlic, and peppers and sauté for about 10 minutes, until softening. Add the pepper mixture to the tomatoes and simmer, covered, for 45 minutes until very soft. Taste and season with salt and pepper.

Preheat the grill or broiler to high. Sprinkle the tuna steaks with olive oil and arrange on a rack over a foil-lined broiler pan. Broil for about 2 minutes on each side, until crusty on the outside and still pink in the middle. Alternatively, barbecue on a rack over hot embers for slightly less time. Serve with the peperonata, which can be served hot or cold.

meat and poultry
carni

broiled sausages
with tomato and sage bean stew
salsicce con fagioli all'uccelletto

1 lb. dried cannellini or haricot beans or,
if lucky, 2 lb. fresh cannellini or borlotti beans

a pinch of baking soda

8 fat fresh Italian-style sausages, or good
butcher's sausages

⅓ cup olive oil

3 garlic cloves, crushed

about 10 sage leaves

12 oz. fresh ripe tomatoes, peeled, seeded,
and puréed, or 1¼ cup passata (Italian sieved
tomatoes)

sea salt and freshly ground black pepper

Serves 4

Tuscans have a reputation for being great game hunters. In the past, when they
used to cook little gamebirds, or *uccelletti*, they would generally season them
with sage. Although this dish contains no *uccelletti*, it is cooked in the same
way—the sausages take the place of the birds. This is the most famous of the
hundreds of ways to cook beans and is equally delicious served with roast
pork—or even a homemade hamburger.

If using dried beans, put them in a bowl, cover with plenty of cold water, and soak
overnight. The next day, drain and rinse, then cook in plenty of boiling water without any
salt, but with the baking soda (to keep the skins soft) for about 1–1½ hours, or until tender.
Drain. If using fresh beans, shell and boil them in slightly salted water until cooked, about
25–30 minutes, then drain.

Preheat the broiler to high. Brush the sausages with oil and place on a rack over a foil-lined
broiler pan. Broil for about 15 minutes, turning occasionally, until tender and crisp on the
outside. Alternatively, barbecue on a rack over hot embers for slightly less time.

Meanwhile, heat the oil in a saucepan and add the garlic, sage, and pepper. Fry until the
garlic is golden and the sage is beginning to become transparent and crisp. Remove
and reserve a few crisp leaves for serving. Add the puréed tomatoes to the pan, heat
to simmering, then add the cooked beans. Cook for 10 minutes, then taste and adjust
the seasoning with salt and pepper. Serve the sausages with the beans. Garnish with the
reserved crisp-fried sage leaves.

meatballs with porcini mushrooms and pecorino
polpette toscane

2 oz. dried porcini mushrooms, soaked in warm water for 30 minutes

1¼ lb. ground beef or veal

1 cup mashed potato or cooked rice

¼ cup freshly grated pecorino cheese

3 tablespoons freshly chopped flat-leaf parsley, plus extra to serve

1 garlic clove, finely chopped

½ cup fresh white bread crumbs

2 tablespoons whole milk

1 egg, beaten

sea salt and freshly ground black pepper

olive oil, for shallow-frying

tomato sauce:

2 tablespoons olive oil

1 small onion, finely chopped

two 14-oz. cans chopped tomatoes, drained

2 tablespoons freshly chopped basil

Serves 4

There are versions of these all over the region and each one is different. The addition of potato and bread crumbs are pure Tuscan thrift. Sometimes the meatballs are dipped in flour or even fine polenta before frying.

Drain the mushrooms and chop them finely. Put in a large bowl with the ground meat, potato, pecorino, parsley, and garlic. Mix together well. Soak the fresh bread crumbs in the milk, squeeze until damp, then add these to the mixture with the egg. Season with salt and pepper and mix well until it begins to come together. Cover and chill in the refrigerator for 30 minutes.

To make the tomato sauce, heat the olive oil in a skillet, add the onion and cook for 5 minutes, until softened. Add the tomatoes and basil and simmer for about 30 minutes, stirring occasionally.

Form the chilled meatball mixture into 8 slightly flattened cakes or balls and shallow-fry in hot oil for about 3 minutes on each side, until cooked through and golden brown. Add the tomato sauce and reheat for about 5 minutes, until boiling. Sprinkle with parsley, then serve immediately.

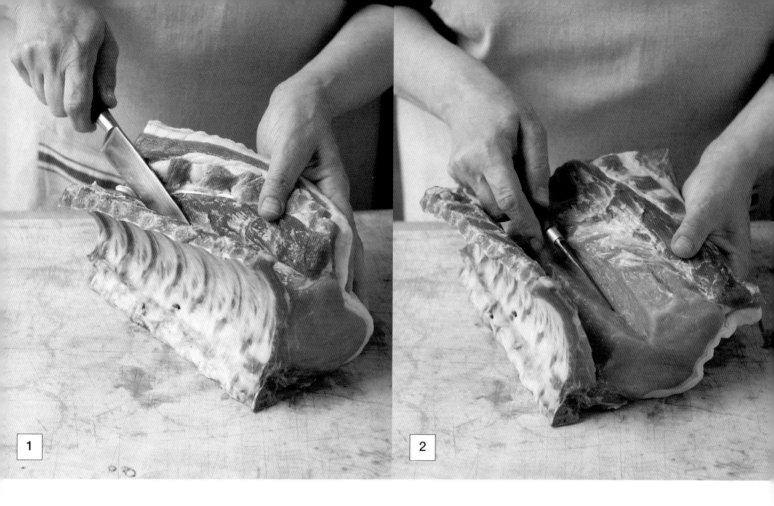

pork loin roasted with rosemary and garlic *arista alla fiorentina*

4 lb. bone-in pork loin roast

4 large garlic cloves

¼ cup finely chopped rosemary

a bunch of long rosemary sprigs

1⅓ cups dry white wine

extra virgin olive oil, for rubbing and frying

sea salt and freshly ground black pepper

kitchen string
a large roasting pan

Serves 6

Redolent of early morning markets in Florence where *porchetta* (whole pigs stuffed with herbs and roasted overnight in wood-fired ovens) is sold sliced and crammed into huge buns as a morning snack. The pan juices make divine gravy.

Make a paste of the garlic, chopped rosemary, at least ½ teaspoon of salt, and pepper in a food processor or spice mill. Set aside.

(1) Using a sharp knife, release the meat from the top of the rib bones working down to the base. (2) Make a deep cut through the eye of the loin. (3) Rub the garlic paste into the cut surfaces of the meat. (4) Close the meat back onto the bone and tie up neatly with kitchen string. (5) Tuck some of the long sprigs of rosemary under the string and along its length.

Weigh the meat and calculate the cooking time, allowing 25 minutes for every pound, plus a final 25 minutes. At this stage, you can wrap it and leave it in the refrigerator for several hours to develop the flavor. When ready to cook, preheat the oven to 450°F.

Unwrap the pork and bring it to room temperature. Set the joint in a roasting pan and tuck the remaining rosemary sprigs underneath. Season. Roast for 20 minutes, then reduce the heat to 375°F and (6) pour half the wine over the joint. Roast for the remaining calculated time, basting the pork with wine every 20 minutes. When cooked, let the pork rest in a warm place for 15 minutes, then carve into thick slices to serve.

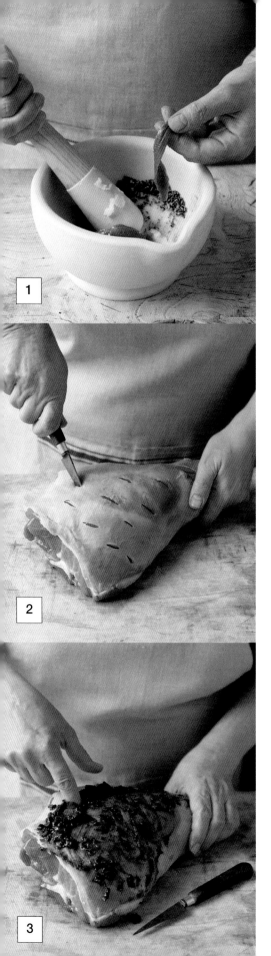

leg of lamb "seven hills of rome"
coscia di agnello "sette colli di roma"

This leg of lamb is braised until cooked and tender, then roasted to color it. The powerful flavorings melt into the meat, with the anchovies disappearing to leave a lingering salty note. This way of cooking lamb stems from the days of the Roman Empire, when the most popular condiment was a sauce made from fermented fish.

3 lb. leg of lamb

2 tablespoons olive oil

10 juniper berries

3 garlic cloves, crushed

2 oz. salted anchovy fillets, boned and rinsed, or canned anchovies

1 tablespoon freshly chopped rosemary

2 tablespoons balsamic vinegar

2 sprigs of rosemary

2 fresh bay leaves

1¼ cups dry white wine

a few sprigs of thyme

sea salt and freshly ground black pepper

a flameproof casserole dish (into which the lamb should fit snugly)

Serves 6

Trim the lamb of any excess fat. Heat the oil in the casserole dish, add the lamb, and brown it all over. Remove and cool quickly.

(1) Crush 6 of the juniper berries, the garlic, anchovies, and chopped rosemary with a mortar and pestle. Stir in the vinegar and mix to a paste.

(2) Using a small, sharp knife, make many small incisions into the lamb.

(3) Spread the paste all over the meat, working it into the incisions, then season with salt and pepper.

Preheat the oven to 325°F. Put the rosemary sprigs and bay leaves in the casserole dish and set the lamb on top. Pour in the wine. Crush the remaining juniper berries and add to the lamb, then add the thyme. Cover, bring to a boil on top of the stove, then braise in the preheated oven for 1 hour, turning the lamb every 20 minutes.

Raise the oven temperature to 400°F. Roast, uncovered, for another 45 minutes or until browned—the lamb should be very tender and cooked through.

Transfer the lamb to a serving dish and keep it warm. Skim off the fat from the pan, then boil the sauce, adding a little water if necessary and scraping up the sediment. Season with salt and pepper if necessary and serve with the lamb.

beefsteak with arugula
tagliata con la rucola

4 T-bone steaks (about 8 oz. each)
2 tablespoons olive oil
8 oz. arugula
sea salt and freshly ground black pepper
freshly chopped parsley, to serve

a ridged grill pan

Serves 4

Italians love meat cooked very rare: you will often see a slip of a girl tucking into a steak that would comfortably feed two—and she will eat it all. The steaks are produced from the huge, handsome, white *Chianina* cattle, native to Tuscany. A great place to taste real Tuscan beef simply cooked over wood embers is at *Ristorante dei Laghi*, near Civitella, which is a carnivore's paradise—family run, warm, and welcoming, and full of hunters' stuffed trophies.

Brush the steaks with olive oil and season very well with salt and pepper. Heat a ridged grill pan until smoking hot. Add the steaks and cook for 2 minutes on each side to seal, then lower the heat and continue to cook for 4 minutes per side for medium-rare steaks, less for rare.

Transfer the steaks to a cutting board, cut the meat from the bone, and slice it thickly. Put a pile of arugula on 4 warm plates and arrange the sliced meat on top. Pour any juices from the steaks onto the meat and serve immediately, sprinkled with chopped parsley.

devilled grilled chicken
pollo alla diavola

1 medium chicken, about 3 lb. 5 oz.

1 cup olive oil

freshly squeezed juice of 1 lemon

2 garlic cloves, crushed

1 teaspoon hot red pepper flakes

sea salt and freshly ground black pepper

lemon wedges, to serve

a mesh grill basket

Serves 4

Chicken and small gamebirds are very popular cooked this way. They are split open and flattened to cook evenly. Tuscans love to cook *alla brace*—over hot coals in the hearth. To make the charcoal brazier, a wood fire is lit, and when the wood has turned to glowing red ashes, they are spread out in an even layer and left until white on top. A low iron grill on legs is set over the braizier and the spatchcocked birds cooked on top. The smell is wonderful as they sizzle over the coals. The cooked spatchcocked bird is said to resemble the shape of the devil's face, hence the name *alla diavola*. The legs resemble devil's horns, the charring is the color of the devil and the red pepper makes it hotter than hell! The best way to eat these is with your fingers.

Take the chicken and turn it breast-side down. You will see the backbone underneath the skin on the base, finishing with the parson's nose. Take a pair of kitchen scissors and cut along one side of the backbone. Cut along the other side and remove the backbone completely. Turn the bird over, breast-side uppermost, and open out. Press down hard on the breast bone until you hear a crack and the bird flattens out.

Mix the olive oil with the lemon juice, garlic, and pepper flakes and add a good pinch of salt and lots of pepper. Pour this into a shallow dish, add the chicken and turn in the marinade to coat. Cover and leave to marinate in the refrigerator for at least 1 hour, preferably overnight.

Preheat the broiler to high or heat a barbecue and wait for the coals to turn white. Remove the chicken from the refrigerator and its marinade and lay it flat on one side of the mesh grill basket. Clamp it shut. Grill or barbecue bone-side first for 20 minutes. Turn the chicken over, reduce the heat and cook for a further 20–30 minutes, until cooked through and blackened, but not burnt. Baste with the marinade from time to time during cooking. Serve piping hot with lemon wedges.

sweet things
dolci

panna cotta
with candied orange peel
panna cotta con spicchi d'arancia canditi

2 cups heavy cream

1¼ cups whole milk

¼ cup superfine sugar

1 vanilla bean, split

3 leaves of gelatin or
3 teaspoons powdered gelatin*

candied orange peel:

2 unwaxed oranges

¼ cup sugar

6 molds, about ½ cup each

Serves 6

*Panna cotta must be wobbly. However, if you are nervous about turning them out, use 4 leaves or teaspoons of gelatin.

The secret of a great panna cotta is in the wobble. I have eaten many indifferent versions—some of them made from packet mixes. This one is really very good. Panna cotta means "cooked or scalded cream" and is said to have originated in Piedmont or Lombardy, where the cream and milk are very rich.

To make the panna cotta, put the cream, milk, and sugar into a saucepan. (1) Scrape in the vanilla seeds, then bring to a boil. (2) Crumble or sprinkle the gelatin into the cream mixture and stir until dissolved. (3) Pour through a strainer.

Cool, then place in the refrigerator until it is JUST beginning to thicken. At this stage, stir the cream briskly to distribute the vanilla seeds. (4) Pour into the 6 individual molds, set on a tray and refrigerate for at least 5 hours, or until set.

To make the candied peel, remove the peel from the oranges with a sharp vegetable peeler (removing any bitter white pith with a knife afterwards). Cut the peel into long fine shreds. Bring a small pan of water to a boil and blanch the shreds for 1 minute, drain then refresh in cold water.

Put the sugar and ½ cup water into a small pan and stir until dissolved. Add the orange shreds and bring to a rolling boil. Boil for 2–3 minutes, then strain the shreds through a sieve, reserving the syrup, and tip onto a plate to cool. Before they cool too much, use your fingers to separate the shreds out a little so that they don't stick together.

When ready to serve, (5) press the top of the panna cottas and gently pull away from the edge of the mold—this breaks the air lock and they should drop out easily. (6) If they don't want to come out, you'll need to dip each mold very briefly into warm water (be warned they will melt if the dipping water is too hot) and then invert onto the plate. (7) Give the mold a good shake. (8) The panna cotta should drop out.

Decorate each panna cotta with the candied orange shreds and a spoonful of the reserved orange-infused syrup.

5

6

7

8

zabaglione

There is nothing quite as sensual as warm zabaglione served straight from the pan. Many like to beat it in a copper bowl so that it cooks quickly. The secret is not to let the mixture get too hot, but still hot enough to cook and thicken the egg yolks. The proportions are easy to remember: one egg yolk to one tablespoon sugar to one tablespoon Marsala, serves one person. It must be made at the last moment, but it doesn't take long and is well worth the effort.

2 large egg yolks
2 tablespoons Marsala wine
2 tablespoons sugar
savoiardi biscuits (ladyfingers), for dipping

Serves 2

(1) Put the egg yolks, Marsala, and sugar in a medium heat-proof bowl (preferably copper or stainless steel) and beat with a hand-held electric mixer or a whisk until well blended.

(2) Set the bowl over a saucepan of gently simmering water—the bottom of the bowl should at no time be in contact with the water. Do not let the water boil. (3) Whisk the mixture until it is glossy, pale, light, and fluffy and holds a trail when dropped from the whisk. This should take about 5 minutes. (4) Serve immediately in warmed cocktail glasses with savoiardi for dipping.

Variation: To make chilled zabaglione for two, when cooked, remove the bowl from the heat and whisk until completely cold. In a separate bowl, whisk ⅔ cup heavy cream until floppy, then fold into the cold zabaglione. Spoon into glasses and chill in the refrigerator for 2–3 hours before serving.

tiramisù with raspberries
tiramisù con lamponi

This amazingly popular dessert is said to have originated in Venice in the 1950s. For added texture, I like to grind real bittersweet chocolate in a blender for layering and sprinkling. Some recipes are too sweet for my taste, but you can add more sugar to the cream mixture if you like. Make this in a large glass dish or in individual glasses and serve for a special occasion.

6 oz. bittersweet chocolate, with over 60% cocoa solids

1¼ cups heavy cream

½ cup Italian espresso coffee

6 tablespoons Marsala wine

8 oz. mascarpone cheese (1 cup)

⅓ cup sugar

2 tablespoons dark rum

2 egg yolks

24 savoiardi biscuits (ladyfingers)

1 pint fresh raspberries, plus extra to serve

a serving dish or 4 good-sized glasses

Serves 4

Put the chocolate in a blender or food processor and grind to a powder. Set aside. Pour the cream into a bowl and whisk until soft peaks form. Set aside.

Pour the espresso into a second bowl and stir in 2 tablespoons of the Marsala. Set aside. Put the mascarpone in a third bowl and whisk in 3 tablespoons of the sugar, then beat in 2 tablespoons of the Marsala and the rum. Set aside.

To make the zabaglione mixture, put the egg yolks, the remaining 2 tablespoons Marsala, and the remaining 2 tablespoons sugar in a medium heat-proof bowl and beat with a hand-held electric mixer or whisk until well blended. Set the bowl over a large saucepan of gently simmering water—the bottom of the bowl should at no time be in contact with the water, and don't let the water boil. Whisk the mixture until it is glossy, pale, light, and fluffy and holds a trail when dropped from the whisk. This should take 5 minutes. Remove from the heat and whisk until cold. Fold in the whipped cream, then fold in the mascarpone mixture.

Dip the savoiardi, one at a time, into the espresso mixture. Do not leave them in for too long or they will disintegrate. Start assembling the tiramisù by arranging half the dipped savoiardi in the bottom of a serving dish or 4 glasses. Trickle over some of the leftover espresso. Add a layer of raspberries. Sprinkle with one-third of the ground chocolate, then add half the zabaglione-cream-mascarpone mixture. Arrange the remaining dipped savoiardi on top, moisten with any remaining espresso, add some more raspberries, and sprinkle with half of the remaining chocolate. Spoon over the remaining zabaglione-cream-mascarpone mixture and finish with a thick layer of chocolate and extra raspberries. Chill in the refrigerator for at least 3 hours (overnight is better) for the flavors to develop. Serve chilled.

granitas and sorbets

Granitas and sorbets are thought to have been introduced to the Mediterranean basin by the Moors during their occupation of Sicily. Snow from Mount Etna was piled into glasses and sweet fruit juices poured over it—a perfect cooler when the hot winds blew over the island. In 1533, Caterina de' Medici brought a Sicilian ice cream-maker to the court of her French husband, King Henry II. It was another Sicilian, Francesco Procopio dei Coltelli, who opened the famous Café Procope in Paris in 1686. His highly-prized sorbetti were made with fruit juice mixed with shaved ice and flavored with jasmine or rose water.

Today sorbets are based on fruit juices or puréed fruit and sugar, often laced with wine or liqueur. These are best made in an ice cream machine so that the ice crystals are continually broken down as the liquid freezes, giving a smooth texture. A *granita* is a gritty ice made with sugar or sugar syrup and either fruit juice or coffee. Homemade granita is frozen in a metal tray with the liquid not deeper than 1¼ inches. The frozen outer edges are continually lightly mashed with a fork into the unfrozen center until you have a pile of icy shards. Granita is usually served in a long-stemmed glass and coffee granita is served with whipped cream.

lemon sorbet
sorbetto al limone

It's worth making a journey to Italy just to taste lemons that have been properly ripened in the sun. Walk through a lemon grove when the glossy green trees are in blossom and the scent is intoxicating. The beautiful leaves can be used like bay leaves or the more exotic Thai lime leaves to impart a lemony flavor to sweet and savory dishes alike. In this recipe I mix the orange with the lemon juice, because it softens the acidity of our un-sunkissed lemons.

1½ cups sugar
finely grated peel and freshly squeezed
juice of 6 lemons, plus 6 whole, medium,
even-sized lemons, to serve
finely grated peel and freshly squeezed juice
of 1 orange

an ice cream machine

Makes about 1 quart, serves 6

Put the sugar and 2¾ cups water in a saucepan with the lemon and orange peels. Bring slowly to a boil, then boil rapidly for 3–4 minutes.

Remove from the heat, and let cool. Meanwhile, strain the fruit juices into a bowl. When the syrup is cold, strain into the bowl of juice. Chill. When cold, churn in an ice cream machine for the length of time specified in the manufacturer's instructions.

Meanwhile, cut the tops off the remaining 6 whole lemons and shave a little off each base so that it will stand up. Scoop out the insides, squeeze and keep the juice for another time. Put the lemon shells and tops in the freezer.

When the sorbet is frozen, fill the lemon shells and set the tops back on. Replace in the freezer until needed. Let soften in the refrigerator for 10–15 minutes before serving.

1

2

ricotta and acacia blossom honey ice cream
gelato di ricotta e miele d'acacia

½ cup acacia honey

16 oz. fresh ricotta cheese

2½ cups low-fat milk

1 vanilla bean, split lengthwise

cubes of comb honey, to serve (optional)

an ice cream machine

Makes about 1.5 quarts, serves 9

This is a very delicate ice cream with the slightly granular texture of ricotta. Acacia honey is sweet and perfumed and a favorite throughout Italy. In late spring, acacia blossoms are collected, dipped in sweet batter, and fried to serve with a dusting of confectioners' sugar. The sweetness of the honey is tempered by a hint of vanilla—the eternal Italian favorite.

(1) In a large mixing bowl, beat the honey into the ricotta. Put the milk in a saucepan and add the split vanilla bean. Bring slowly to a boil, stirring occasionally, remove from the heat, and let infuse for 10 minutes. Shake the vanilla bean around in the milk to flush out the seeds then remove it. (2) Pour the hot vanilla-infused milk on the ricotta and honey mixture, whisking well to mix. Let cool and refrigerate for at least 1 hour or overnight.

When thoroughly chilled, transfer the mixture to an ice cream machine and churn for the length of time specified in the manufacturer's instructions. If necessary, you can do this in 2 batches, keeping one batch refrigerated while freezing the other batch. Spoon into a chilled container. Cover and freeze for at least 4 hours until firm.

Remove to the refrigerator for 30 minutes before serving, to soften. Serve scooped into cones or bowls or refreeze in individual molds. Top with the cubes of comb honey, if using.

Cook's note: Gelato or ice cream is always best made in an ice cream machine to give it a lovely creamy texture.

Italian chocolate truffles
tartufi al cioccolato

5 oz. bittersweet chocolate, 60–70% cocoa solids

6 tablespoons salted butter, cubed

1 egg yolk

2 tablespoons Mozart Black Chocolate Liqueur or dark Crème de Cacao

1 teaspoon truffle honey or a drop of real truffle oil (optional)

unsweetened cocoa, to dust

a baking sheet, lined with nonstick baking parchment

Makes about 15 truffles

Look at the picture opposite and you will understand why a chocolate truffle is called a truffle—because it looks very like its dark and earthy savory sibling, the black truffle, and is just as precious to chocoholics. This is a classic truffle recipe—very rich and dense, and reliant on the best-quality chocolate that you can find. For real truffle addicts, stir a little truffle honey or a drop of real truffle oil into the mixture—the flavor combination is quite mysterious but delicious!

(1) Finely chop the chocolate and put it in a clean, dry, thick heat-proof basin (ideally Pyrex). Fill a saucepan one-quarter full of hot water and bring to a simmer (never let the water boil). Fit the bowl snugly into the rim of the saucepan so that it is suspended over the simmering water, and no steam can escape around the sides. The base of the bowl must not touch the water or the chocolate will overheat. (2) When melted, remove the bowl from the heat and stir the chocolate gently until it is completely melted.

Beat in the butter, then the egg yolk, liqueur, and truffle honey, if using. Cover with plastic wrap and refrigerate for about 1 hour, or until set.

Sift some cocoa onto a plate or into a bowl. (3) Using two teaspoons, scoop the chilled chocolate mixture into rough mounds and put them on the prepared baking sheet. Shape each one into a knobbly truffle shape in your hands. (4) Drop into the cocoa and roll each one around until it is completely covered then return to the baking sheet. Layer in an airtight container between sheets of nonstick parchment paper and refrigerate for up to 5 days or freeze for up to 1 month.

lemon and almond tart
torta di limone e mandorle

shortcrust pastry:

2 sticks butter

2 cups all-purpose flour

½ cup sugar

2 egg yolks

lemon and almond filling:

4 extra-large eggs, lightly beaten

⅔ cup sugar

finely grated peel and freshly squeezed juice of 3 lemons

1 stick unsalted butter, melted

¾ cup ground almonds

whipped cream, to serve

a loose-based fluted tart pan, about 9 inches diameter foil and baking beans

Serves 8

A refreshing change from the classic French *tarte au citron*. The almonds give the tart more body and add another flavor dimension. Traditionally, this is made with freshly ground almonds, because they have a fine, creamy texture and a better flavor than the ready-ground kind, which are difficult to find in Italy. If you'd like to try this method, grind the same weight of whole blanched almonds with half the sugar to prevent them becoming oily. Beat the eggs with the remaining sugar, then stir in the ground sugar and almond mixture.

To make the shortcrust pastry, (1) rub the butter into the flour and sugar until the mixture looks like grated Parmesan cheese.

Put the 2 egg yolks in a small bowl, add 1 tablespoon water and beat lightly. (2) Pour into the flour mixture and mix with a round-bladed knife until it looks like chunks of Parmesan.

(3) Tip out onto a clean work surface and knead lightly until smooth. (4) Knead into a ball, flatten, then wrap in plastic wrap and let rest for 30 minutes.

Preheat the oven to 375°F.

(5) Roll out the pastry on a floured surface. (6) Pick up on the rolling pin and use to line the tart pan. Use a small ball of excess pastry wrapped in plastic wrap to push the pastry into the pan. (7) Roll the rolling pin over the pastry to cut off the excess. (8) Prick the base all over with a fork, then chill or freeze for 15 minutes to set the pastry.

Line the pastry case with foil, flicking the edges of the foil inwards towards the center so that it doesn't catch on the pastry. Fill with baking beans, set on a baking sheet, and bake blind in the center of the preheated oven for 10–12 minutes. Remove the foil and beans and return the pastry case to the oven for a further 5–7 minutes to dry out completely.

To make the filling, put the eggs, sugar, lemon peel, and juice in a bowl and whisk together until light and fluffy. Stir in the melted butter and almonds. Mix well and pour into the prepared pastry case. Bake in the preheated oven for 25–30 minutes, until the crust and the top of the tart are golden brown. Remove from the oven, let cool, then chill in the refrigerator before serving in slices with whipped cream.

1   2   3   4

grandmother's cake
torta della nonna

1½ sticks unsalted butter, softened

1 cup confectioners' sugar

2 egg yolks

finely grated peel of 1 orange

1 teaspoon vanilla extract

a small pinch of fine sea salt

1⅔ cups all-purpose flour

custard filling:

2¾ cups whole milk

2 egg yolks

⅓ cup sugar

¼ cup all-purpose flour or cornstarch

½ teaspoon vanilla extract

beaten egg, to glaze

¼ cup pine nuts

confectioners' sugar, to dust

a loose-based tart pan,
9 inch diameter
foil and baking beans

Serves 8

Everyone in Italy knows this fabulous cake filled with pastry cream and topped with crunchy pine nuts. All grandmothers have their own secret recipe and there is a chocolate-flavored version called *Torta del Nonno* (Grandfather's Cake) —to make this delicious variation, substitute 3 tablespoons cocoa for 1 tablespoon of flour for the total flour quantity when making the custard.

To make the pastry, put the butter and sugar in a bowl and beat together until pale and creamy. Beat in the egg yolks, orange peel, vanilla extract, and salt. Work in the flour until almost mixed. Transfer to a work surface and knead gently until smooth. Cut into 2 pieces, one slightly bigger than the other. Form into disks, wrap in plastic wrap, and chill for at least 30 minutes. Roll out the larger piece as thinly as possible and use to line the tart pan. Prick the base of the tart with a fork and put in the freezer for at least 15 minutes.

Preheat the oven to 350°F.

Line the tart with foil, fill with baking beans, and bake in the preheated oven for 15 minutes. Remove the beans and foil and return to the oven for 10 minutes to dry out. Remove from the oven and let cool. Leave the oven on.

Meanwhile, to make the filling, heat the milk until just about to boil, then take off the heat. Beat the egg yolks and sugar in a bowl, then beat in the flour. Pour the milk onto the flour mixture, then whisk well. Return the mixture to the pan and heat gently, stirring until thickening. When it reaches a very slow boil, let boil for 2 minutes, then stir in the vanilla extract. Pour into the cooled pie crust. Let cool.

When cold, roll out the remaining dough to a circle slightly larger than the diameter of the pan. Brush the edges of the crust with beaten egg and cover with the dough circle, pressing it firmly onto the cooked edges and trimming the excess. Brush the dough with more beaten egg and sprinkle with the pine nuts. Using a skewer, make a couple of air holes in the top. Bake in the still-hot oven for 1 hour, then remove and let cool completely. Dust with confectioners' sugar and cut into slices to serve.

soft almond cookies
ricciarelli

6 oz. whole blanched almonds, finely ground
or 6 oz. ground almonds

1 cup superfine sugar, plus extra for rolling

½ teaspoon baking powder

1 tablespoon all-purpose flour

1 large egg white

2–3 drops bitter almond extract

confectioners' sugar, sifted, to serve

Makes 16–20 biscuits

These delicate cookies, with their soft almond centers, are said to resemble the almond-shaped eyes of the Madonna in Renaissance paintings. They are associated with the Feast of the Annunciation on March 25th, and consequently, with fertility. I use whole blanched almonds as they taste fresher when ground.

Preheat the oven to 400°F.

Put the ground almonds in a bowl with the superfine sugar. Sift the baking powder with the flour into the almonds and sugar. In a separate, grease-free bowl, whisk the egg white until stiff but not dry, (1) then stir into the almond mixture.

(2) Add the almond extract and blend until you have a soft malleable paste. Pour some superfine sugar onto a plate. (3) Roll the paste into long sausages, then cut into fingers. Roll each one in superfine sugar, then (4) press into the traditional oval or diamond shape by tapering the ends, then flattening slightly with the palm of your hand.

(5) Arrange the *ricciarelli* on a baking sheet (preferably lined with baking parchment to prevent over-browning). Bake in the preheated oven for 10–12 minutes, until pale golden. They will puff and spread a little. Do not overbake or they will be too hard. Transfer to a wire rack to cool. Press the tops into confectioners' sugar or simply roll in confectioners' sugar and pile high on a plate.

how to make italian coffee

Coffee made in this Napoletana was my first taste of coffee made in an Italian kitchen when I was growing up in Scotland. My mother ran a kitchen shop with her friend Vera who was married to the Scottish/Italian artist Alberto Morrocco. Alberto's father and mother left Italy for a new life in Scotland, and had settled in Aberdeen where they made and sold ice cream. Vera donned the mantle of the Italian wife (as instructed by Alberto's mother), and our family celebrations together at their house were unforgettable. Vera always made coffee in Napoletanas—no matter how many of us there were. I remember the smell and the clatter of them to this day. I find this a gentler brew than coffee made in the popular Moka.

First, open the coffee maker, remove the top cover, then separate the two parts by holding the bottom firmly and lifting the top upwards. Pull out the central filter and unscrew the filter cover. (1) Fill it with finely ground espresso coffee.

(2) Fill the part of the coffee maker without the spout with water (the water level should be just below the little steam hole at the top.)

(3) Screw the filter cover back on. (4) Reinsert the central filter.

(5) Place the part with the spout on top of the base unit as if it was a cover.

The coffee maker is now ready to be placed on the heat, setting the part without the spout on the burner. For best results, the unit should be placed to the side of the burner rather than over the center, to avoid burning or damaging the handles.

When steam exits from the little hole, this signals that the water is boiling; at this point, remove the coffee maker from the heat source and (6) quickly turn it upside-down, making sure that you hold both handles tightly as you do so.

The boiling water will start to filter through the coffee. Wait 2–3 minutes for the coffee to brew and stop dripping, then serve.

the napoletana coffee maker

We don't all have an electric espresso maker at home, so a Napoletana is the next best thing. The Napoletana was THE domestic model in Italy long before the advent of the Moka and the espresso machine in the 1950s. It is a stove-top coffeemaker that both brews coffee and acts as a serving pot. In fact, the humble Napoletana was such a part of Italian life, the Alessi company commissioned Italian designer Riccardo Dalisi to redesign it for the modern age. His researches lasted nine long years (1979–1987) producing more than 200 prototypes, now lodged in the Alessi museum. The final result in 1987 was an incredibly elegant (and expensive) polished stainless steel reincarnation.

To me, it makes better coffee than a Moka because it's impossible to overheat or burn the coffee grounds which gives a bitter taste. When the boiled water in the base is turned over and allowed to drip through the coffee, it produces a mellow yet full-bodied cup of coffee. There are no rubber rings to replace and no fizzing valve to terrify you! My traditional aluminium Napoletana came from a street market in Italy, but they can be found in good kitchen shops and online (for details of stockists see page 192).

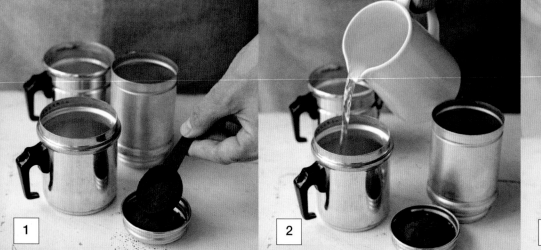

1 2

3

glossary of Italian ingredients

ANCHOVIES *(acciughe, alici)*

Whether salted or in oil, these are essential to give a deep savoriness to some Italian dishes, especially those from the South. They have been a firm favorite since Roman times.

Salted anchovies (*acciughe sotto sale*) are the whole fish (without heads) preserved in salt, and need to be split open, backbone extracted, and rinsed. Available in jars or larger cans, salted anchovies have a fresher taste than the fillets preserved in oil (*filetti di acciuga*). They look better, as they retain their silvery skin. Both can be soaked in milk or water to soften them and remove excess salt.

BALSAMIC VINEGAR *(aceto balsamico)*

Aceto balsamico tradizionale is a rich, sweet vinegar from Modena, made from the boiled-down must of white Trebbiano grapes, which is then aged in wooden casks for at least 10 years and some of the best for as much as 60 years. The price does reflect the quality. As the vinegar ages, it becomes richer and sweeter, and storing it costs money!

Balsamic vinegar is especially good sprinkled on strawberries, and can enrich a sauce or salad dressing. There is no real substitute, but sherry vinegar reduced with a little sugar would do at a pinch. Cheaper versions made with vinegar and caramel are available but cannot be called *aceto balsamico tradizionale*.

BLACK PEPPER *(pepe nero)*

Black pepper is extensively used in Northern Italian cuisine due to the influence of the spice trade through Venice. It is always used freshly ground—the aroma is incredible. Never buy ready-ground pepper—it will be stale. Combined with salt, pepper flavors many a preserved meat and sausage. It is one of the spices used in the medieval sweetmeat from Siena – *panforte*.

BOTTARGA *(uova di tonno)*

This is tricky to find even in Italy, and very expensive. It is the salted, pressed, and dried roe of the tuna or grey mullet and is an acquired taste—you either love it or hate it. It tastes of concentrated salty dried fish and is used sparingly (grated) to dress pasta or when very fresh, it is thinly sliced and served with a squeeze of lemon juice.

Tuna *bottarga* is found in Southern Italy and Sicily while mullet *bottarga* is to be found in Sardinia. It is sold by weight in a piece or ready-cut and vacuum-packed. It is also found in small jars, dried and finely grated like Parmesan, to mix into pasta with chile, garlic, and parsley. Always bring some back when visiting Italy—it freezes well.

BREAD CRUMBS *(pangrattato)*

There is no waste in an Italian household, and bread is no exception. Leftover bread is dried and made into bread crumbs—an essential part of Italian cuisine from the North to the South. Fried in butter or oil, they are the Parmesan of Southern Italy and known as *la mollica*.

CAPERS *(capperi)*

These are the unopened flower buds of a leathery-leaved Mediterranean plant, which grows readily in the poorest of soils in the wild and by the coast. The buds are hand-picked, dried, and preserved either layered in coarse salt or in vinegar. Both types should be well-rinsed before using, and can be soaked in cold water for a while to soften the flavor. Caper berries are the seed-pods if the flowers are left to fruit. Preserved in the same way, they are served as a garnish with cold meats and cheeses. The best capers are said to be the smallest, and come from the islands of Pantelleria and Salina near Sicily.

CHEESE *(formaggio)*

Parmigiano (**Parmesan**) is a hard *grana* (grainy) cheese. It is salty and crumbly, and a pale straw color. *Parmigiano Reggiano* is the best, but **Grana Padano** is cheaper and just as good in cooking. Although adding Parmesan shavings to salads is "fashionable," it is normally finely ground. It is used liberally in northern cuisine, especially in *risotti* but it is a cardinal sin to use it on or with seafood.

Pecorino is also a hard, *grana* (grainy) cheese that can be used in the same way as Parmesan. In Italy, pecorino is the generic name for cheeses made from pure sheep's milk. Each cheese is characteristic of a specific area and of a particular breed of sheep.

Mozzarella is traditionally made from buffalo milk, but the majority is made with cow's milk. It is snowy white when fresh, and springy. It is usually sold sitting in its own whey to keep it moist. Tiny balls of mozzarella are called *boccocini* and are perfect wrapped with Parma ham and served with *aperitivi*.

Mascarpone is a fresh, thick cheese made from cream (like cream cheese, but with a richer flavor and smoother texture), and it is used in and with desserts.

Ricotta is a cheese made from whey which is re-cooked and should be snowy white and sweet—it is also sold in a harder salted version, good in salads. It can be made from cow or sheep's/ewe's milk (*ricotta di pecora*). *Ricotta di pecora* is extensively used in Sicily and the south and is a by-product from making pecorino.

CHILES *(peperoncini)*

Both dried and fresh chiles are used in abundance, especially in the south and in Tuscany (a cure for an upset tummy is boiled rice mixed with chopped chile). Italians use dried chile flakes when fresh is not available. The heat of the chile depends on the season and the variety—remove the seeds for less heat, and use disposable latex gloves if you don't want to be burnt or get "chile eye!"

DIGESTIFS AND LIQUEURS
(digestivi e liquori)

These are normally consumed at the end of a meal and after coffee to aid digestion, or just to end the whole meal on a high! They are usually infusions of alcohol, herbs, fruits, and/or spices mixed with sugar syrup. Italians are very fond of **amaro**—a thick, dark bittersweet infusion of beneficial herbs, spices, bitter orange, sugar, and alcohol—of which there are many brands, notably **Fernet Branca**. You will either love it or hate it and it is said to be a good hangover cure! Iced **Limoncello** is a happy way to end a meal, especially if you are offered the homemade variety. It is the essence of Southern Italy in a liqueur—lemons macerated in sugar and pure alcohol—heavenly! Sweet almondy **Amaretto** is very popular, but I find it a bit sickly and use it for cooking only. Then there is the minefield that is **Grappa** a spirit distilled from wine grape must (this can be from a single grape variety), then aged and flavored with whatever takes your fancy—myrtle berries in Sardegna and even the bitter herb *ruta* (rue). Anything aniseed is adored for its tummy-settling properties, syrupy yellow **Strega** being one of them along with the the colourless feisty **Sambuca**, served poured over a coffee bean of *mosca* (fly) on the bottom of the glass, not on the top... and never flamed. However, some waiters can get carried away if given a good reception and that is part of the joy of Italy!

DRIED AND CANDIED FRUIT
(uva passa e frutta candita)

Uva passa are raisins, and golden *Sultanina* raisins are found in Sicily, along with the truly amazing, enormous, muscat-like *Zibbibo* raisins from Pantelleria. Currant-like **Uvetta** are used in desserts and savory dishes alike.

Frutta candita is candied whole fruit and thick slices of lemon, orange, and citron peel are used with abandon in desserts and cake-baking—this delicacy was brought by returning Crusaders to mainland Italy, and by the conquering Moors to Sicily. As a general rule, the further south you go in Italy, the sweeter the tooth!

DRIED WILD MUSHROOMS
(funghi porcini secchi)

The most famous and prized mushroom is the **porcino**. They are gathered in the woods during the autumn months and much coveted. **Dried porcini** come in different grades—slices, pieces, and broken pieces, and are priced accordingly. They must be eaten within a year of drying and are stored in an airtight jar. Soak in warm water for 30 minutes before using—keep and strain the soaking water, it will add loads of flavor to a sauce, soup, or stew.

FLOUR (farina)

There are two main types of flour used throughout Italy. **Farina di Grano Tenero**, which is the finest, whitest grade of soft wheat flour ("00" and "0" indicates the grade of the flour—"00" being the finest) and **Semola di Grano Duro**, a hard wheat semolina flour. It is made from the heart of the wheat so has a higher gluten and protein content. *Semola* is used in commercial dried pasta, eggless pasta, Sicilian breads, and pizza. This flour gives pasta a firmer texture and is the best choice for dusting fresh pasta to prevent sticking—it is coarser and so falls off the pasta during cooking. Finer *semola rimacinata* is used for bread-making as it is twice-milled.

Couscous is a Sicilian speciality, and is still hand-rolled from two grades of semolina flour. It is eaten with a fish broth.

Chick pea flour (farina di ceci) is mainly used to make the street foods farinata in Liguria and Tuscany and *panelle* (chickpea fritters) in Sicily.

FLOWER WATER (estratto di fiori)

Orange flower water, rosewater, and jasmine water were assimilated into Sicilian cuisine during the Moorish occupation, and are used to delicately perfume sweets, pastries, salads, and desserts. They are especially good with almonds.

GARLIC (aglio)

Garlic is used in many ways to give a vast range of flavors. The larger the cloves (and heads) of garlic, the sweeter it will be, especially if still purply green and fresh. Small hard heads of garlic tend to be bitter and strong. The softer and fresher the garlic, the more subtle the flavor. When frying garlic, be careful not to let it color too much or it can go bitter.

HERBS (erbe)

Although fresh herbs are an essential part of Italian cooking, **oregano (origano)**, a wild form of marjoram, is best used dried for optimum flavor. Big aromatic bunches appear in local markets during the season —crumble it from the stems between your fingers to release the aroma. The leaves and flowers are crumbled and sold in bags when the season is over. Most other herbs are used fresh not dried. **Bay leaves (alloro)** and **mint (menta)** are used copiously in Sicily. **Parsley (prezzemolo)** is generally the flat-leaf variety and used in abundance. **Basil (basilico)** of course is essential and grows on every Neapolitan balcony. **Sage (salvia)** and **rosemary (rosmarino)** are the Tuscan herbs. **Tarragon** has the wonderful Italian name **dragoncello** and is better used fresh than dried. **Nepitella** is a type of wild catmint used with mushroom dishes, especially in Tuscany and Sicily.

ITALIAN SAUSAGE (salsiccia)

Freshly made in Italian delis (or to order in Italian pork butchers) *salsiccia* are made with coarsely ground pork (two thirds lean and one third fat) highly seasoned with salt and pepper. They are often flavored with fennel seeds, chile, basil, and pine kernels. They are best roasted over wood embers or on the grill. They are firm and juicy and have loads of flavor. Sometimes they are wound into a coil to cook in a skillet or on the grill to be sliced into wedges. *Luganega* is the most famous type of *salsiccia*, originating from Lombardia.

NUTS *(noci)*

Pine nuts *(pinoli)*, the seeds of pine cones from the Mediterranean stone pine, are expensive, as their extraction is labor-intensive. They are not toasted—they are used to add a creamy sweetness.

Walnuts *(noce)*, hazelnuts *(nocciole)*, and almonds *(mandorle)* are all used extensively in Italian desserts and sweets, as well as to thicken sauces and soups. Fresh chestnuts *(castagne)* are roasted over open fires to munch with new red wine, and candied for desserts.

Dried chestnuts make wonderful soups and stews and when ground into a sweet flour, are used to make the Tuscan speciality, the sweet chestnut and rosemary cake *Castagnaccio*, or to flavor some pastas and gnocchi.

OLIVES *(olive)*

Olives are a much-prized crop throughout Italy, picked from September when green, or left to ripen on the tree until purple then black and picked in winter. The flavor is dependent on the time they are picked. Fresh green olives are very acid and bitter and are pricked and brined before preserving in oil. Green and black olives suit different dishes, and are not really interchangeable. Olives are, of course, crushed to make olive oil. Black and green olive pastes are rich and salty and can be used as toppings, bread and pasta flavorings, or even whisked into a dressing.

OLIVE OIL *(olio d'oliva or uliva)*

Olive oil is essential to Italian cuisine, and the choice is limitless—some are peppery, some grassy and some have a hint of almond. There are six grades of cold-pressed olive oil, the finest being *olio d'oliva extra vergine* (extra virgin olive oil up to 1% acidity) for dressing salads and drizzling over meat or soups, and the quality is expressed in the price. Use a lighter, less expensive oil like *olio d'oliva vergine* (virgin olive oil up to 3.5% acidity) for cooking and baking. A dark green olive oil does not necessarily guarantee quality, it depends on the type of olive used—taste it and see. Buy the best olive oil you can afford for drizzling and dressing and a cheaper one for sautéing. Keep it in a dark, cool place—the fridge or cool pantry is best. It may solidify, but leave it out in the room for a couple of minutes to loosen up. It should be consumed within a year of pressing—it can go rancid. Contrary to popular belief, olive oil is used for deep-frying as it reaches a high temperature before breaking down.

PANCETTA

Pancetta is unsmoked cured belly pork (*pancia* is Italian for stomach). There are two kinds—**pancetta stesa** which is the whole piece, and **pancetta arrotolata**, which is seasoned, spiced, rolled, and matured, then sliced to order—it is a dry cure and smoked bacon should not be substituted. **Pancetta affumicata** is cured and smoked and very thinly sliced like fat-streaked bacon slices.

PASTA

Dried pasta *(pasta asciutta)*

Dried pasta can be made with egg (*all'uova*) or without egg. It is the staple food of southern Italy (from Naples downwards) where it is commercially made from durum wheat (*grano duro/semola*) and water only. There are hundreds of shapes, all named differently according to regions, and there is even a pasta museum in Rome!

Fresh pasta *(pasta fresca)* is made with eggs and "00" soft wheat flour and is made and eaten in the North, especially Emilia-Romagna. This is the pasta to use for making ravioli, tortellini, and other filled pastas. It has a wonderful silky texture.

POLENTA

This poor peasant food of the North is enjoying a global revival! Coarsely ground maize or corn (*granoturco*) is used to make either soft polenta to serve with rich meat sauces, or the firmer sliced and grilled polenta, to serve with roasted meats and game. You would think that polenta was just polenta, well think again—different regions and even different cities have their own preferences. Coarser grades are preferred in Bergamo and Verona. In Tuscany, Lazio, and Abbruzzo, they prefer a soft polenta made with fine maize meal. Polenta in Venice and Friuli is a finer grade and milled from delicate white maize (*polenta bianca*).

Polenta takes a good 40 minutes to cook with continual stirring, but quick-cook or instant polenta, cooking in 5–10 minutes works well, although the texture and flavor of the real thing is best. Wrapped-up, firm polenta keeps for about two days in the refrigerator. You can buy ready-made stuff in a vacuum pack, but it has a disappointing flavor and texture.

PROSCIUTTO

Prosciutto is the generic term for ham. **Prosciutto crudo** is raw cured ham, and **prosciutto di Parma** is a particularly high quality *prosciutto crudo*. If you ask for prosciutto in a shop in Italy, they will always ask "*crudo o cotto?*"—raw or cooked.

PULSES AND BEANS *(legumi e fagioli)*

Beans are all staple foods throughout Italy but especially in Tuscany (so much so that the Tuscans are known as *mangiafagioli*, literally bean-eaters!). **Fresh beans** used include **fave** (young fava beans)—they are devoured raw in late spring with *pecorino* or *prosciutto crudo*—and **borlotti**, the beautiful red-marbled beans that sadly lose their coloring when cooked. All fresh beans have a lovely creamy texture when cooked and are packed with protein.

Dried beans, including borlotti, haricot, black-eyed beans, cannellini, and toscanelli are used throughout southern Italy during the winter to make soups and purées.

Dried chickpeas *(ceci)* are amongst the oldest foods still eaten in Italy—they are cooked in soups, salads, and stews, and must be well-soaked before using. Try not to buy old stale ones—they will never cook!

Lentils *(lenticchie)* are also widely used in Italian cooking. The finest and smallest come from Castelluccio in Umbria. They are eaten on New Year's day for good luck. Generally they don't need soaking unless they are very old.

RICE *(riso)*
The array of rice on an Italian supermarket shelf is truly astounding! It is used in *risotti*, timbales, soups, salads, Sicilian *arancini* (rice balls), and Roman *supplì* (croquettes). There are four types of rice grown in the Po Valley. *Ordinario* (short round grain used in desserts), *semifino* (medium-length round grain for soups and salads), *fino* (long grain for everyday use), and *superfino* which is the best for *risotti*. *Arborio*, *Vialone Nano*, and *Carnaroli* are all superfino—they have good absorption and plenty of starch, essential for making delicious, creamy *risotti*.

SALT *(sale)*
Salt is extremely important in the Italian kitchen. Pasta water is liberally salted to give the pasta flavor, and all fried food should be sprinkled with salt as soon as it comes out of the oil. Everything is seasoned during the cooking process, so that the salt can penetrate deep into the food and release the flavors. In Italy sea salt, still made by the ancient method of evaporation in open pans. **Fine salt** *(sale fino)* is used for the table and baking, and **coarse salt** *(sale grosso)* used in cooking. Much of Italy's salt comes from Sicily, where it is made in the same stone salt pans built

by the Greeks. Bleached naturally in the sun, the huge white mountains are then protected by overlapping terra cotta tiles.

SPICES *(spezie)*
The ancient Romans used wild fennel and poppy seeds to flavor breads, but it was during the Renaissance when Venice was the center of the spice trade with the East, that spices came to be widely used.

Cinnamon *(cannella)*, **nutmeg** *(noce moscata)*, **vanilla** *(vaniglia)*, **aniseed** *(anice)*, **cloves** *(chiodi di garofano)*, **ginger** *(zenzero)* were used to show wealth, mask the taste of tainted food and as preservatives. They are all still used today, especially in the Veneto, Siena, and Sicily, in baking and both sweet and savory dishes. **Juniper** *(ginepro)* is prized in mountain country and around Rome. **Fennel seeds** *(semi di finocchio)* and **saffron** *(zafferano)* grow wild in southern Italy and Sicily and became fundamental to the cuisine.

TOMATOES *(pomodori)*
Although a newcomer to Italian cuisine from the New World in the 16th century, tomatoes have become an essential ingredient, especially in Naples and the south. They come in all shapes and sizes from long **plum** to **cherry**. Really ripe red tomatoes are used for sauce-making, whereas the greenish under-ripe tomatoes are eaten in refreshing salads. They are so cheap that Italians still bottle them whole and make sauce for the winter.

Canned and **bottled tomatoes** are essential when fresh are not available—at least they have seen the sun! A pinch of sugar will correct the acidity.

Passata is sieved crushed tomatoes, thicker than tomato juice, but not nearly as thick as purée. It can really pep up a sauce or stew.

Tomato purée or **paste** *(concentrato di pomodori)* comes in jars, cans, and tubes and must be refrigerated once opened. This is essential to the

storecupboard to add depth of flavor to sauces and stews.

Sicilian **strattú** or **estratto**, a rusty red "clay" of puréed, salted and sun-dried fresh tomatoes is a real find—a little goes a long way and it keeps for months. Succulent tomatoes are puréed and sieved, mixed with salt and lightly cooked. The thick sauce is spread over wooden boards and left to dry in the scorching sun. The sauce is scraped and turned until it has turned to bright red "clay" then it is rolled into balls and stored under olive oil. Commercially-made *estratto* is a reddish brown, and doesn't quite have the zing of the hand-made stuff. Look in Sicilian markets and some enlightened delis and bring some back when on holiday, but wrap it well and keep in the refrigerator (it keeps in the freezer too).

Sun-dried tomatoes are actually used sparingly in Italy. They originate from the South, where they are traditionally halved, salted and left in the sun to dry out on woven fennel stalk mats. They are also commercially dried. The reddest, flexible ones will have the best flavor and can be used to boost sauces, soups and stews.

TRUFFLES *(tartufi)*
The **Alba truffle** is the most prized of all **white truffles** *(tartufi bianchi)* for its pungent aroma and flavor, and is eaten raw. The best come from Piemonte, and they also can be found in the Crete Senese in Tuscany and in the Veneto. **Black truffles** *(tartufi neri)* come from Norcia or Spoleto in Umbria. Fresh truffles are unbelievably expensive. Truffles in jars are nothing like the real thing and not worth the high price. **White truffle paste** is a good standby, and small jars of truffle and mushroom paste are treats to mix into pasta or spread onto crostini. **Truffle oil** can enhance a risotto or grilled meat, but it is powerful so use judiciously. When buying, check that it really has seen a real truffle and isn't a ghastly chemical creation—these are to avoided at all costs!

index

websites and mail order

conversion charts

Weights and measures have been rounded up or down slightly to make measuring easier.

Volume equivalents:

American	Metric	Imperial
1 teaspoon	5 ml	
1 tablespoon	15 ml	
¼ cup	60 ml	2 fl.oz.
⅓ cup	75 ml	2½ fl.oz.
½ cup	125 ml	4 fl.oz.
⅔ cup	150 ml	5 fl.oz. (¼ pint)
¾ cup	175 ml	6 fl.oz.
1 cup	250 ml	8 fl.oz.

Weight equivalents:		**Measurements:**	
Imperial	Metric	Inches	Cm
1 oz.	25 g	¼ inch	5 mm
2 oz.	50 g	½ inch	1 cm
3 oz.	75 g	¾ inch	1.5 cm
4 oz.	125 g	1 inch	2.5 cm
5 oz.	150 g	2 inches	5 cm
6 oz.	175 g	3 inches	7 cm
7 oz.	200 g	4 inches	10 cm
8 oz. (½ lb.)	250 g	5 inches	12 cm
9 oz.	275 g	6 inches	15 cm
10 oz.	300 g	7 inches	18 cm
11 oz.	325 g	8 inches	20 cm
12 oz.	375 g	9 inches	23 cm
13 oz.	400 g	10 inches	25 cm
14 oz.	425 g	11 inches	28 cm
15 oz.	475 g	12 inches	30 cm
16 oz. (1 lb.)	500 g		
2 lb.	1 kg		

Oven temperatures:

110°C	(225°F)	Gas ¼
120°C	(250°F)	Gas ½
140°C	(275°F)	Gas 1
150°C	(300°F)	Gas 2
160°C	(325°F)	Gas 3
180°C	(350°F)	Gas 4
190°C	(375°F)	Gas 5
200°C	(400°F)	Gas 6
220°C	(425°F)	Gas 7
230°C	(450°F)	Gas 8
240°C	(475°F)	Gas 9